I0776717

The Creatures of Midnight

MAXIMO D. RAMOS

PHOENIX PUBLISHING HOUSE
927 Quezon Avenue, Quezon City

Contents

Preface

FILIPINO CHILDREN often frighten their little brothers and sisters by saying, "Here comes the *nuno*!" Long ago the word *nuno* did not just mean an old man. It also meant a dwarf of storyland.

Some of our parents still say, "A nice girl must not sing or fall asleep in the kitchen while she is cooking supper." They say that the girl who does either of these will marry an old man. Did you know that the old man they meant was not a person but a legendary dwarf?

More questions

Have you observed that some mothers and their daughters refuse to sweep the floor at noon or about sunset? And can you tell why Filipinos love to eat sour, salty, and spicy foods?

Many Filipinos still believe that we have an eclipse when a large dragon of the sky swallows the sun, the moon, or both. During an eclipse some Filipinos shout and beat on drums and tin cans. They say this is to frighten the big dragon and make it spit out the sun and the moon and then the world will be filled with light again.

Have you seen houses with stuffed globefish or empty shells of large crabs hanging from the eaves? Has your mother ever asked you to move away from a post while you were asleep or never to sleep at the center of the floor? Have you ever heard old people tell young men and women not to marry in a hurry? Do you know why?

Our ancestors believed many things about the unseen creatures of the Philippine storyland. If you have a good storyteller at home, he may have told you interesting legends about these creatures. And you may have asked a lot of questions about them which he could not answer. If you want to know more about these creatures, turn the pages of this book, look at the pictures, and enjoy what is said about the creatures.

What this book is about

This book tells about 85 creatures of legend. Many people believe that they exist and are afraid of them. But these creatures do not really exist. They are in our minds but not around us.

We call them creatures of midnight because it is said that they show themselves to people about the middle of the night. By the places they live in, the things they do, and what they look like, these creatures are like most of the creatures in stories from Europe. They have many different names, but they can be put in twelve groups:

demons	merfolk
dragons	ogres
dwarfs	vampires
elves	viscera suckers
ghouls	weredogs
giants	witches

The Devil is not told about in this book. For there was no Devil in our old legends and myths. The Devil is new to the Filipinos. It was probably brought into this country by the Europeans.

There are no fairies in the Philippine storyland. The fairies you have loved in European tales have kings, queens, and knights and their ladies, and they live in cities in the deep woods. They live in palaces and pretty gardens. There are no kings, queens, and knights and their ladies among the Philippine creatures of midnight. There are no fine palaces and pretty gardens in our forests. Few of these creatures live in groups bigger than the family.

But as you will learn from this book, there are creatures in Philippine legends that are somewhat like the European fairies. These are the elves. There are many pretty elves in the legends our ancestors told. These elves have no kings and queens. They have no knights and their ladies. But it is said that they live in fine houses and cities. Their homes look like large trees to us, and their cities look like dark groves.

Many of us still believe that elves exist. Before we climb a tree, gather its fruit, or cut it down, we still say, "Excuse me!"

Why we should get to know these creatures

Our ancestors had many beliefs about the creatures of midnight. A lot of our grandparents believed they existed. But these creatures are fast being forgotten. They are getting fewer and fewer. We have to tell about them in books. Then you and I and those who come after us will know the creatures our ancestors believed in and enjoyed or feared. Children in other lands enjoy tales about dragons, dwarfs, elves, giants, merfolk, ogres, and witches. Through books they learn not to fear these strange creatures. You, too, should enjoy our creatures of storyland and learn not to fear them.

Today we thank God for a good harvest from our farms. But some farmers still believe that friendly dwarfs living in anthills give them good crops. Our farmers must learn to destroy anthills and plant more rice where the anthills stand. It is not true that dwarfs live there.

Lower and higher creatures of storyland

The beings that we will tell about in this book are creatures of lower mythology and in tales. They are so called because they are said to be mostly harmful.

The creatures of higher mythology are the good gods and goddesses that people tell legends about. Two of the creatures of higher Philippine mythology are Lumawig and Bathala. Ghosts are creatures in higher myths and in tales, too. So are angels, but there are no angels in Philippine legends.

I hope that after you get to know these creatures of lower Philippine mythology better, you will never fear them again. I hope, too, that you will enjoy the exciting legends told about them.

And I hope that after you get to know more about these creatures, you will help enrich Philippine life and culture by weaving the beliefs about them in your games, dances, songs, stories, poems, and pictures.

From The Publisher

MAXIMO D. RAMOS, the first editor in chief of Phoenix Publishing House, was associated with the company from 1963 until his death on December 12, 1988. As editor and consultant, he gathered together a team of teachers who were creative, understood the needs of Filipino students, knew their pedagogy, and, above all, were committed to the ideals of nationhood espoused by my father, Dr. Ernesto Y. Sibal.

The present leadership of Phoenix Publishing House in the textbook field in all subject areas on all three levels of the educational system is due, in a large measure, to the unfaltering loyalty and passion for work of Dr. Ramos.

Dr. Ramos never relaxed his own personal pursuit of the Muse and continued to write short stories, poems, and essays. At the same time, he devoted special attention to serious research on Philippine mythology and folklore. All these were done as he taught and performed administrative duties at the Philippine Normal College and later at the University of the East.

Phoenix Publishing House takes pride in publishing these ten volumes of the essential works of Dr. Ramos. We know that his legacy will fire the imagination of Filipino students and inspire them to know more about their own folkways and folklore and to write them down for others to enjoy and appreciate. Dr. Ramos's only limitation perhaps is access to Filipino language as medium of his literary output. But he has shown the Filipino student that one can master the English language and use it to advantage in portraying Philippine reality. And because the setting is Filipino and the experiences are part of the Filipino tradition, we know that his writings will appeal to children and to adults as well.

His works, collectively titled REALMS OF MYTHS AND REALITY, consist of the following:

<ol type="I">
<li>TALES OF LONG AGO IN THE PHILIPPINES</li>
<li>PHILIPPINE MYTHS, LEGENDS, AND FOLKTALES</li>
<li>LEGENDS OF LOWER GODS</li>
<li>THE CREATURES OF MIDNIGHT</li>
<li>THE ASWANG COMPLEX IN PHILIPPINE FOLKLORE</li>
<li>PHILIPPINE DEMONOLOGICAL LEGENDS AND THEIR CULTURAL BEARINGS</li>
<li>BOYHOOD IN MONSOON COUNTRY</li>
<li>PATRICIA OF THE GREEN HILLS AND OTHER STORIES</li>
<li>REMEMBRANCE OF LENTS PAST AND OTHER ESSAYS</li>
<li>THE CREATURES OF PHILIPPINE LOWER MYTHOLOGY</li>
</ol>

This collection is our tribute to Dr. Maximo D. Ramos and our contribution to Filipiniana.

J. ERNESTO SIBAL
Publisher

The Demons

The demons in Philippine myths are like tall, dark men. They live in big trees with thick and rounded leaves. They live in *balete* and *kalumpang* trees. The flowers of the kalumpang smell bad, but people are afraid to cut the tree down. They are afraid of the demons living in it.

The demons are big and frightful to see. There is fire in their mouths. Some of them have burning jewels to play with. They smoke cigars that don't burn out. But they are afraid of fire.

They grow bigger and bigger. Then they grow smaller and smaller. They change themselves to carabaos that have no horns. They change themselves to horses, pigs, dogs, cats, and roosters. They even change themselves to a ball of fire. They appear and disappear. Their ears are not pointed and they have no horns or fangs. Sometimes they have no heads at all.

People who are frightened when they see a demon become insane.

Some of the Philippine demons are

    allawig (*Ilokano*)
    ani-ani (*Zambal*)
    bangungot (*Tagalog*)
    bantay (*Pangasinan*)
    baras (*Pangasinan*)
    kapre (*Bikol, Ilokano, Tagalog*)
    lagtaw (*Tausug*)
    mutya (*Ilokano, Tagalog*)
    pugot (*Ilokano, Pangasinan*)
    santilmo (*Ilokano, Tagalog, Visayan*)
    sarangay (*Ibanag*)
    talahiang (*Zamboangan*)
    tikbalang (*Tagalog*)

The Allawig

Ilokanos call it *allawig*, and Pangasinenses *silew-silew*.
It is a ball of fire that doesn't burn things.
It is blue, green, orange, red, or yellow.
It is round and not pointed at the top like fire.
It flickers dimly or flames out brightly.
It is found in fields and swamps where no one lives.
It moves ahead of people who travel by night.
A traveler who follows it loses his way.
Tha allawig leads him around and around.
He follows it and walks in circles, too.
Then the allawig leads him to a pit.
He falls into the pit and dies.
Or it leads him to a swamp.
He sinks in the swamp and drowns.
He should take off his clothes and wear them inside out.
Then the allawig will vanish and he will find his way
    home.

Gorio and Kulas are walking home one night.
They see a fire ahead of them.
How can they tell that it is an allawig?
_________ They walk in circles.
_________ The fire doesn't burn the grass.
_________ The fire runs after them.

The Ani-ani

The Zambals
    call him *ani-ani.*
He looks like a man
    eighteen feet tall.
His legs are like
    two large wooden posts.
He is strong and heavy
    and moves slowly.
He is black, hairy,
    and sometimes bearded.
He has a large flat nose
    and a wide mouth.
His lips are thick
    and his skin is rough.
His fingers are large, with sharp nails.
He comes out when the moon is new.
He sits smoking on the branch of a tree.
He blocks the path of a traveler at night.
He has a strong goat smell.
He changes from a man to a beast.
Then he changes from one beast to another.

Why does the ani-ani change its size and shape?
    _____ *Perhaps to try to escape.*
    _____ *Probably to frighten people who see it.*
    _____ *Maybe to make people laugh.*

The Bangungot

The Tagalogs call it *bangungot*.
The Ilokanos call it *batibat*.
It looks like a very fat dark man or woman.
It lives in a hole in a house post.
It lived in that hole when the post was still a tree.
It didn't leave the hole when the tree was cut down.
It sits on the chest of people who sleep near the post.
It sits on those who ate too much.
They shout, but their voice doesn't come.
They can't breathe because the bangungot is heavy.
They have a bad dream and sometimes choke to death.
Don't shout when a bangungot is choking you.
Bite your thumb and wiggle your big toe instead.
Then the bangungot will leave you.
It will run into its hole in the post.

A girl had a bad dream one night.
A big fat creature sat on her chest.
She tried to scream, but her voice did not come.
What was perhaps the real cause of her bad dream?
_____ She ate too much and had indigestion.
_____ The bangungot sat on her chest.
_____ She went to sleep near a post.

5

The Bantay

Pangasinenses know him as *bantay*.
He looks like an old man living in a large tree.
He turns into a great big white rooster.
It grows smaller and then bigger.
It lives in a large tree by the river.
It comes out of the tree on dark nights.
It comes out when the moon is new.
It comes out when there is a light shower.
It doesn't let people go near the tree.
It blocks their way so they can't pass.

A farmer is walking home from his farm one night.
He sees a big rooster under an old tree.
What will he probably do?
    ____ *Turn back and take another road.*
    ____ *Go straight ahead.*
    ____ *Fight the bantay.*

The Baras

He is called *baras* in Pangasinan.
He is called *kalariot* in Pampanga.
He is called *kirbas* among the Ilokanos.
He lives in the deep woods.
He is tall, dark, and hideous.
He comes into the village late at night.
He opens a window and gets in.
He carries off the pretty maiden who is asleep.
He carries her off to his house in the woods.
She wakes up in his house and sees him.
Then she is frightened and becomes insane.

Why do barrio folks close their windows at night?
_____ There are thieves.
_____ It is dark.
_____ They are afraid of the baras.

The Lagtaw

To the people of Sulu, it is
    called *lagtaw*.
It is tall, black, and big like
    other demons.
Its large eyes are like fire.
Its nose and ears are large.
It lives in great big trees.
Its legs are like ship masts.
It lives inside a tree hole.
It leaves its hole at night.
Then it goes out to frighten
    boys and girls.

Salih sees a lagtaw one night.
What can he expect the lagtaw to do?
    _____   *Change into an animal.*
    _____   *Eat him up.*
    _____   *Grow bigger and then smaller.*

The Kapre

He is *kapre* to Bikolanos and Ilokanos.
Pampangos, Tagalogs, and Visayans call him kapre, too.
Arabs call him *kafir* and Spaniards *cafre*.
He is as tall as the tree beside which he stands.
He grows shorter and then taller.
He looks like a man but smells like a goat.
He becomes a large cat, pig, or carabao.
So Ibanags call him, *ammalabi*, "the ever-changing one."
His skin is dark, rough, and hairy.
He has big ears and thick lips.
His eyes are as large as saucers.
He has a flat nose and a big mouth.
He appears under a new moon and a soft shower.
He smokes a big cigar that doesn't grow shorter.
If you are brave, tie a rope around his neck.
Then tie the rope to a tree.
Next morning dig under the tree unseen by anyone.
Dig in the ground at the end of the rope.
You will find a jar of gold there.

What did Linda probably do when she saw a kapre?
_____ Smiled and said, "Good Evening."
_____ Shouted for help.
_____ Closed her eyes and ran.

The Mutya

It is called *mutya* in many parts of the country.
Its name is *moya* in Palawan.
Its name is *muya* in India, meaning 'jewel' or 'pearl'.
It is a magic ball of fire.
Many plants and animals have a mutya.
The gabi has a mutya that keeps a person dry.
The nightjar has a mutya that keeps one unseen.
Hunt for a banana flower that is about to bend.
The flower will bend to the ground at midnight.
Stand under the flower with your mouth open.
The mutya will drop when the flower bends.
It will drop from the end of the banana flower.
Catch the jewel in your mouth.
Then put it underneath your tongue.
A tall dark creature will try to snatch it
    from you.
It will wrestle with you and choke you.
It will carry you into the air.
It will frighten you with its ugly face.
It will frighten you with its burning eyes.
Don't you be afraid of the creature.
Keep the jewel underneath your tongue.
If you are frightened, you will go crazy.
If you are brave, you will be the strongest
    of men.

Who probably owns the mutya?
_____   *A demon.*
_____   *The banana tree.*
_____   *The night.*

The Pugot

He is called *pugot* by Ilokanos and Pampangos.
He looks like a tall, dark man.
He lives in large trees with big oval or round leaves.
These trees are the *apatot, bangar, bittaog,* and *lugo.*
He is headless and sometimes armless.
His name *pugot* means dark or headless.
He has a strong, unpleasant smell.
He courts the pretty girls in the village.
He frightens their human suitors away by stoning them.
He changes his size and shape before them.
He becomes a headless, tailless pig, dog, goat, or cat.
Fire gets out of his cut throat.
But he is afraid of fire.

Poldo sees a tall man walking toward him one night.
What will he probably do?
_____ Run and meet him.
_____ Strike a match and walk home.
_____ Stand right where he is.

The Santilmo

Tagalogs, Visayans, and other Filipinos
    call it *santilmo*.
It is a ball of fire in fields and swamps.
It bounces along and rolls away.
It changes into a beast with fire in its
    mouth.
Travelers and fishermen follow it at night.
They walk and walk till they are tired out.
Then they cannot find their way home.
They walk into deep mud and thorny
    bushes.
They get dizzy and become insane.
They must reverse their clothes to
    send it away.
Then they can find their way home.

*Two villagers see an ember on their
    path.*
*It bounces along the grass but does
    not burn it.*
What will they probably do?
    ____ *Walk and walk.*
    ____ *Sit down and rest
    a little.*
    ____ *Wear their clothes
    inside out.*

The Sarangay

The Ibanags call him *sarangay*.
Like other demons he is tall and dark.
He has a large body, too.
His hair is long, coarse, and black.
He wears big wooden rings on his ears.
He lows like a bull and runs after boys and girls.
He owns a magic jewel.
His jewel glows like an ember in the dark.
A man who steals it grows as strong as ten.

Anton meets a dark stranger one night.
The stranger grows bigger and bigger.
There is a fire in the stranger's mouth.
What will Anton perhaps do?
_____ *Hurry home.*
_____ *Pray to the stranger.*
_____ *Throw a stone at him.*

The Talahiang

People in Zamboanga call him *talahiang*.
He is twelve feet tall and has large muscles.
He is dark and has coarse, kinky hair.
He has thick lips and large teeth.
He lives in big trees in the jungle.
He makes travelers lose their way.
But he is afraid of noise.
He runs away when he hears a shout.
He changes himself into a big lizard and flees.

Tinoy sees a talahiang high up in a tree.
The talahiang says, "Come here, boy."
What can he do?

    _____ *Beat two sticks together.*
    _____ *Shout at the top of his voice.*
    _____ *Stone the talahiang.*

The Tikbalang

To Tagalogs he is called a *tikbalang*.
To Negritos he is a *tuwung* and to Visayans a *tayho*
He has a horse's hairy head and neck.
He has round hoofs, long legs, and large teeth.
He has a man's body and arms.
He makes people follow him and lose their way.
He wears red clothes and makes himself look
    like one's relative.
He frightens people till they grow crazy.
Mount the tikbalang if you are brave.
Snatch three golden hairs from the top of his head.
He will fly up into the sky with you.
He will fly over fields, mountains, and seas.
He will fly to the moon and among the stars.
Hold on to your seat and never fear.
He will grow tired and bring you back home.
Then he will be your faithful servant.
He will plow your fields and plant your crops for you.
He will run errands for you.
He will make you rich and powerful.

What are the chief traits of the Philippine demons?
_____ *They are tall and dark.*
_____ *They try to frighten boys and girls.*
_____ *They eat people.*

The Dragons

Long, long ago, our ancestors believed that there were dragons. Some of the dragons were big and others were small. The bodies of the dragons had parts from different kinds of beasts. Their bodies were those of snakes or crocodiles. Their heads were those of lions, tigers, eagles, or sharks. And their powerful wings were like the wings of eagles.

Some of the dragons lived in the sky. Others lived on land or in the sea. Still others lived both on land and in the sea.

The early Filipinos believed that the crocodile and the python were dragons. Many Filipinos still think that crocodiles and pythons are dragons.

Our ancestors believed in four kinds of dragons. Some of these were

1. birdlike dragons
   a. bawa (*West Visayan*)
   b. laho (*Pampango, Tagalog*)
   c. minokawa (*Bagobo*)
2. fishlike dragons
   bakunawa (*West Visayan*)
3. crocodile-like dragons
   buwaya (*Ilokano, Tagalog, and others*)
4. snake-like dragons
   a. mameleu (*West Visayan*)
   b. markupo (*West Visayan*)
   c. sawa (*Tagalog*)

The Bakunawa

The West Visayans called it *bakunawa* long ago.
It had the body of a great big shark.
It had the gills of a great big fish.
Its mouth was as large as a lake.
It had coarse whiskers and a red tongue.
It had wings, big and small, on its sides.
It lived in the deepest part of the ocean.
Sometimes it flew up into the sky.
Then it caught the sun or moon in its big mouth.
It swallowed them and the world became dark.
So the people below said there was an eclipse.
They were afraid and they made lots of noise.
The bakunawa heard the noise and was frightened.
He let the sun or moon go.
Then the sun shone bright in the sky again.

Why did people make a noise during an eclipse?
_____ They were happy.
_____ They were afraid.
_____ They were hungry.

The Bawa

The West Visayans of early times called it *bawa*.
The bawa looked like a very large bird.
It lived in a cave high above the clouds.
Its cave was hidden behind a curtain of blue smoke.
When hungry, it flew out of its cave.
Then it swallowed the sun or the moon or both.
The people on earth were frightened.
They were afraid the bawa would come down.
Then it would eat them all.
They played sweet music on the mountains.
"Let go of the sun and moon!" they sang.
"We will give you nice food to eat if you do."

What should you do during an eclipse?
_____ *Watch it through darkened glass.*
_____ *Run home crying.*
_____ *Sing a song to the bawa.*

The Buwaya

It is called *buwaya* all over our country.
The buwaya is a crocodile.
But Tagalogs and Visayans thought it was a dragon.
They thought it carried a big box on its back.
It lived in a cave in deep water.
It caught people in the water.
Then it put them in the box on its back.
It took them to its cave in the water.
The people prayed to the buwaya.
They called it *nuno* or "grandfather."
They gave it food when they saw it.
The chiefs punished people who killed it.

You see a buwaya in the water one day.
What should you do?

　　　_____　　*Hit it with a stick.*
　　　_____　　*Run away to safety.*
　　　_____　　*Pray to it.*

The Laho

Long ago Pampangos and Tagalogs called it *laho*.
Its name is from *rahu*, a Hindu word.
The *rahu* was a dragon in the myths of India.
It swallowed the moon and caused eclipses.
Our ancestors were frightened during an eclipse.
They thought a dragon had just swallowed the moon.
"Nilamon ng laho ang buwan!" the Tagalogs shouted.
Many people in Asia and the Pacific area still think so.
The word *laho* still means darkness in Pampango and
    Tagalog.

The children were playing under the moon one night.
By and by, part of the moon grew dark.
Soon the moon became red.
What should the boys and girls have done?
    ____   *Watched the eclipse.*
    ____   *Gone on playing.*
    ____   *Shouted that the dragon*
                 had eaten the moon.

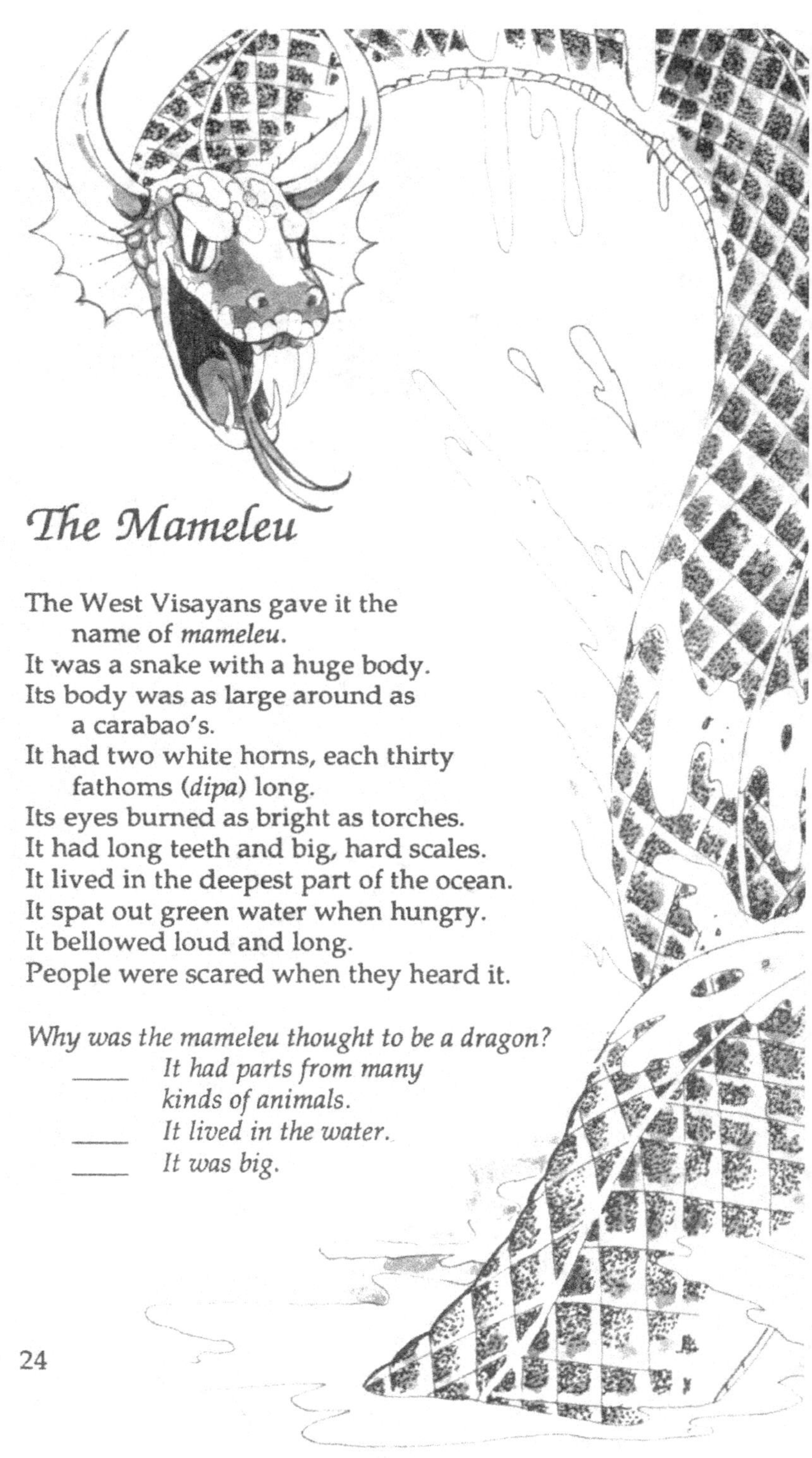

The Mameleu

The West Visayans gave it the
    name of *mameleu*.
It was a snake with a huge body.
Its body was as large around as
    a carabao's.
It had two white horns, each thirty
    fathoms (*dipa*) long.
Its eyes burned as bright as torches.
It had long teeth and big, hard scales.
It lived in the deepest part of the ocean.
It spat out green water when hungry.
It bellowed loud and long.
People were scared when they heard it.

Why was the mameleu thought to be a dragon?
    _____   *It had parts from many*
            kinds of animals.
    _____   *It lived in the water.*
    _____   *It was big.*

The Markupo

West Visayans of long ago called it *markupo*.
It had the body of a very large snake.
A red crest stood on its head.
Its tongue was long and had thornlike hairs.
It had two white tusks in its mouth.
Its long tail was split at the tip.
It lived on top of a mountain
    in the West Visayas.
There it sang a loud song
    on quiet nights.
People feared it, for its breath
    was poison.
Men and beasts died if the markupo
    breathed on them.
Trees became poisonous if it breathed
    on them.
Birds died if they sat on the poisoned trees.

What are the main traits of the Philippine dragons?
        ____ They can change their
        shape and size.
        ____ Their bodies look like
        parts of various animals.
        ____ They can swallow large objects.

The Dwarfs

The Philippine dwarfs look like old men. They never grew since they were two or three years old. They have large heads. They have large eyes, noses, and mouths, too. Their ears are big and round. They cannot see clearly but can hear well. Their hands and feet, their elbows and knees, are large. Their beard is long and thin.

They wear red or brown clothes. They wear a salakot made from dried *upo* fruit. They wear basket hats, too.

They live in their homes under the ground. They have jars of gold, rubies, sapphires, emeralds, and diamonds there. They come out of their homes at noon and about sunset. They pass by magic through the holes in termite mounds.

They visit our yards and premises at noon and about sunset. We mustn't sweep our floors or our yards when the dwarfs are around. If we do, we might sweep dirt into their large eyes. Then they will make us blind.

We can't see them and so we sometimes step on them or hurt them. Then they will punish us. They will pinch us, give us skin disease, and make us sick with chills and fever. They will turn our mouth to one side. They will kill us if we seriously hurt them.

We must ask for their permission when we pass by anthills or cross fields where few people go. We must tell the dwarfs to keep off before we throw water or rubbish out of our windows.

Dwarfs are said to own all the land there is. We should pay them rent before we till the land. The rent they will take is boiled white chicken and rice cakes. We have to offer this rent before planting and after harvest. We have to put the food in the field or under the trees after sunset. The food must have no salt, spices, or seasoning, for dwarfs hate these. The rice must be boiled soft, for dwarfs have few teeth. Our crops will be poor if we don't pay rent to the dwarfs who own the land.

Dwarfs are said to steal boys and girls who have nice names and sweet voices. They take them to their homes under the ground. They marry the pretty girls they steal. So children mustn't dress well, have pretty names, or sing in the fields. Girls mustn't sing in the kitchen while cooking supper.

Some of the Philippine dwarfs are these:

ansisit (*Ilokano*)

aran (*Ibanag*)

duwende (*Tagalog, Visayan, and others*)

kalanget (*Ifugao*)

laman lupa (*Tagalog*)

lampong (*Ilongot*)

matanda sa punso (*Tagalog*)

omayan (*Mandaya*)

muntianak (*Bagobo*)

taong-lupa (*Tagalog and Visayan*)

tianak (*Tagalog*)

The Ansisit

The Ilokanos call him *ansisit*.
He is an old man who is as short as a boy of three.
His joints, belly, head, eyes, nose, and mouth are large.
He lives underground and owns all the land.
He lives in caves and anthills, too.
Anthills are mounds of earth made by termites.
He naps on the anthill at noon.
He does not want farmers to plow the ground with
    tractors.
He fears that plowing with heavy tractors will ruin his
    home.
He visits people's yards after the sun has set.
He walks under our homes at noon and after dark.
He doesn't want us to sweep our yard or floor then.
If we do, the dust may get into his eyes.
He pinches us, and our skin becomes blue.
He pulls our toes and makes them twice as long.
He gives us scabies, fever, and chills.

What will Laura do so the dwarf won't pinch her?
    _____ *Take a nap at noon.*
    _____ *Shout when others are napping.*
    _____ *Play in caves and on anthills.*

The Aran

Ibanags call him *aran*.
He is as short as a child
    of two or three.
But he has an old man's
    face, skin, and toes.
He cannot see too well,
    but his hearing is good.
He has long, reddish hair.
His feet are wide and point backward:
His heels are in front and his toes are behind.
He steals rice and courts pretty village girls.
He visits a girl and says he wants to marry her.
If she agrees, he will take her to his home.
His beautiful home is under the ground.
He has plenty of gold and precious stones there.
Pretty girls must wear necklaces of garlic or
    crocodile's teeth.
They must have plain names, like Kanuta
    and Osang.
Then the aran will not court them.

Why must pretty girls have plain names?
    _____ *So they will not be proud.*
    _____ *So the aran will not think they are pretty.*
    _____ *So their names are easy to write.*

The Duwende

Tagalogs and Cebuanos call him *duwende*.
His name comes from the Spanish word
    duende, 'dwarf'.
He is known as *kama-kama* among Ilonggos.
He is a little man with short arms and legs.
But he has large joints, hands, and feet.
His fingers are long and bony.
His fingernails are long and hard, like horns.
His skin is brown and rough.
His face is round and his cheeks are high.
His eyes are large, round, and sharp.
His mouth and teeth are large.
His voice is high-pitched, like
    an old man's.
He lives under an anthill or in
    a cave.
He punishes children who go
    and play there.
When passing by, we must say,
    "Excuse me, sir. I can't
    see you, so please get out of the way."

How should people treat a duwende?
    ______   *Rudely.*
    ______   *Politely.*
    ______   *Cruelly.*

The Kalanget

The Ifugaos call him *kalanget*.
The Gaddangs call him *karanget*, the Ibanags *karango*.
He is called *taong-lupa* or "man of the earth," too.
Sometimes he is called *kutong-lupa* or "louse of the earth."
He is a short old man with a large head.
He lives under ant mounds in the woods and fields.
He is said to be the real owner of all the land.
Farmers can only rent the land from him.
They pay him a rent to plant crops on the land.
The rent is in the form of good food.
He will take food that has no salt or spices.
He hates ginger, pepper, and vinegar.

A farmer wants to plant rice.
How will he probably begin?
     _____ *Offer chicken and cakes to*
             the dwarf.
     _____ *Start plowing right away.*
     _____ *Burn the grass in the field.*

The Lampong

The Ilongots and Ilokanos call him *lampong*.
He is a short old man of the woods and fields.
He has bright eyes and a long, sparse beard.
He is a shepherd of wild deer.
He turns himself into a deer and stands still.
Hunters shoot at him but cannot hit him.
The deer run away while the hunters
    try to shoot him.
Then he turns into an old man again.
He walks away from the hunters.

Why does the lampong turn himself into a deer?
    ____ *To make fun of the hunters.*
    ____ *To help the deer escape.*
    ____ *To run after the hunters.*

The Matanda
sa Punso

The Tagalogs call him *matanda sa punso* and *nuno*.
Matanda sa punso means 'old man of the anthill'.
Nuno means 'grandfather' or 'old man'.
His beard is long but it is not thick.
His nose is low, like a Filipino's.
His ears are not pointed but big and round.
His shirt and pants are red, and he wears a salakot.
He lives under a tree or under a termite mound.
He has plenty of gems and gold in his house.
He keeps his treasure in big jars.
He steals pretty girls from the village.
He offers them jewels and gold to live with him.

Merta is walking by an anthill one day.
She sees a little man on the anthill.
What will she probably say?
        _____ *"Excuse me, please."*
        _____ *"Get out of my way, you."*
        _____ *"Go to work, Old Man."*

34

The Tianak

The Tagalogs call him *tianak*.
The Bagobos call him *muntianak*.
He is called *pontianak* in India.
He is a dwarf like the matanda sa punso.
One of his legs is longer than the other.
He makes himself look like a cute baby.
He lies under a tree and cries.
"Uwah! Uwah! Uwah!" he cries.
Pick him up and he quickly becomes an old man.
Then he has sharp eyes and a long beard.
His skin is wrinkled and brown.
He bites you and runs away.
He laughs and shouts, "I fooled you!"

Which traits describe the Philippine dwarfs?
_____ *Small and old.*
_____ *Dwellers under the ground.*
_____ *Fond of pretty girls.*

The Elves

The Philippine elves are handsome beings in legends. They are often small in size, but some of them are taller than most Filipinos. Their skin is light and they have hair the color of rice straw. Some elves grow dark and ugly after they get people to marry them.

The elves live in trees large and small. They forbid people to climb or cut down their trees. People must get their permission to gather fruit. People who offend them become ill.

The Philippine elves live in families. But they seldom live in larger communities. Unlike the fairies of Europe, the Philippine elves have no kings, queens, and courtiers. They hold no dances and parties under the trees. There are no fairies in Philippine legends.

Some of the elves speak to people in whistles. They tease people by hiding their things or by stealing their food. But they give their human friends useful gifts, such as magic pots and purses.

These are some of the Philippine elves:

aghoy (*East Visayan*)
dalakitnon (*East Visayan*)
dayamdam (*Agusanon*)
enkantada, enkanto (*Bikol,Tagalog, Visayan*)
kiba-an (*Ilokano*)
kamanan-daplak (*Zambal*)
lewenri (*Romblomanon*)
palasekan (*Ilongot*)
ragit-ragit (*Romblomanon*)
tamawo (*West Visayan*)
tirtiris (*Ilokano*)
ugaw (*Pangasinan*)

The Aghoy

The East Visayans call them *aghoy*.
They look like little men and women.
Their skin is fair and smooth.
They have deep-set eyes, blue, green, or brown.
They have high noses and yellow hair.
Their feet are bare and they dress like villagers.
They live in trees near villages.
They come into a village after dark.
They speak to men in whistles.
They make friends with kind people.
They give their friends wonderful gifts.
They give them magic pots always full of food.
They give them magic purses always full of gold.

Juan was walking in the fields one windy day.
He heard someone whistle to him.
He looked and looked, but no one was there.
What could it really have been?

    ______   *A bird.*
    ______   *An elf.*
    ______   *A split bamboo.*

The Dalakitnon

They are called *dalakitnon*
    by the East Visayans.
Their name means
    'those who live in the *balete* tree'.
They appear like good-looking
    tall men and women.
Their skin is smooth and white.
Their hair is wavy and brown.
Their clothes have gold and silver threads.
They mix with people and attend public dances.
They go to college and travel in foreign lands.
They drive new cars and win beauty contests.
But they live deep in the wild woods.
What we think are balete trees are their mansions.
We hear the clink of dishes in their kitchens.
We smell their cooking and hear their babies cry.
An attractive city girl once came to the village.
She wanted to spend a quiet summer near a forest.
A good-looking youth met her at the village dance.
They danced and danced, and she fell in love.
She agreed to visit his folks.
In his car he drove her to a beautiful city.
The streets were wide and the houses were splendid.
Next morning she was found weeping in the woods alone.

To the barrio folk, who could the stranger have been?
        ____ *A city boy vacationing in the village.*
        ____ *A dalakitnon who fooled her.*
        ____ *A rich admirer from the village.*

39

The Dayamdam

They are known as *dayamdam* in Agusan.
They are the tiniest folk you have ever seen.
Their noses are high-bridged and thin.
Their hair is straight and thin, too.
They hop about on fallen trees in the woods.
They cover themselves with leaves.
They stick out their tongue at you and hop off.
They own every tree in the deep woods.
We must ask their permission to gather fruit.
We must get their permission to fell forest trees.

A woodsman wanted to cut down a tree.
How did he probably begin?
    _____ *Took a nap under the tree.*
    _____ *Said, "May I cut down this tree, sirs?"*
    _____ *Built a fire under the tree.*

The Enkantada and Enkanto

They are called *enkantada* and *enkanto* in Northern
    Mindanao, the Visayas, and Southern Luzon.
The words are Spanish and mean 'the enchanted ones'.
They are blond and handsome mythical people.
They are tall, straight, and brown-haired.
Their noses are high, narrow, and long.
But they have no philtrum, the canal on people's upper
    lips.
They live in large trees, chiefly the balete.
Their trees are mansions with lighted rooms and mirrors.
They dance, hold parties, and listen to music there.
They smell as sweet as the flowers in the green woods.
They are afraid of spicy food.
We know they are near when we smell the scent of
    wild flowers.
The enkantada seduces the village young men.
The enkanto seduces the pretty village girls.
They become ugly and dark after people
    marry them.
Then their victims find it too late to escape.

A pretty woman of the woods courted a farmer.
He wanted to know if she was human.
What did he probably do to find out?
   _____   *He married her.*
   _____   *He offered her spicy food.*
   _____   *He looked to see if she*
                had a philtrum.

The Kiba-an

Ilokanos call them *kiba-an*.
They resemble people but are just a foot tall.
Their long wavy hair extends to their feet.
They have sharp eyes and gold teeth.
They light their path with their shiny teeth.
They sing with sweet, high-pitched voices.
They live in trees swarming with fireflies.
They cook fish and greens in their tree kitchens
    at sunset.
We can smell their cooking as we pass by.
Their food smells like crushed leaves and grass.
They are giving birth when the sun shines through rain.
They steal rice from people's bins.
They steal fish from people's bamboo traps.
They steal hair from children's heads.
They can change themselves to bamboo stakes.
Then they pretend they are part of a bamboo fence.
Their tiny footprints point the other way,
    their toes behind and their heels before.
They give their friends magic pots and purses.

Someone has been stealing fish from my trap.
I see tiny footprints pointing north.
Where did the thief probably go?
     _____   *East or West.*
     _____   *North.*
     _____   *South.*

The Kamanan-daplak

The *kamanan-daplak* are elves among the Zambals.
They are tiny and cute mythical people.
They smell sweet like ilang-ilang blossoms.
They have long hair the color of corn tassels.
They live in trees over mountain brooks.
They live the same way people live.
They call people by name at sundown.
People hear their names called and they wonder.
For they see no one there at all.
They are kind to infants who are left alone.
They put sweet wild flowers beside them.

Marta went to the woods one day.
Someone called her, "Marta, Marta."
She looked and looked, but no one was there.
What did she probably do?

    _____ *She hurried home.*
    _____ *She said, "Here I am."*
    _____ *She looked some more.*

The Lewenri

They are called *lewenri* in Romblon.
They are tall and handsome and fair of skin.
They wear clothes of violet, black, and white.
They mix unseen with people in the village.
They show themselves to the lonely traveler.
They appear to boys and girls by moonlight.
They appear to them at dawn, noon, and
    sunset, too.
They make frightful and shrill sounds.
They play sad or joyful music.
They laugh and cry and sing.
They help the humble and punish the proud.

You meet a lewenri one evening.
What will you probably see him wearing?
    _____   *A jacket the color of an orchid.*
    _____   *A coat the color of kamia.*
    _____   *A dress the color of young guava leaves.*

The Palasekan

They are known to the Ilongots as *palasekan.*
They live in trees near human villages.
They speak to people by whistling to them.
They love to hear music made by people.
They are friendly to good men and women.
They warn travelers against danger.
They help friendly farmers raise crops.
They help friendly hunters in the woods.
But they grow angry when people cut down their
    tree-homes.
They can be appeased by a cup of cane-juice wine.

The school year was about to end.
The boys and girls were studying for the final tests.
A whistle came from the dark trees.
One of the boys said it was the palasekan.
He said the palasekan wanted to hear the radio.
Who probably whistled?
_____ The elf who wanted to
*   hear some music.*
_____ The teacher.
_____ Another boy.

The Ragit-ragit

They are known as *ragit-ragit* in
    Romblon.
They are tiny, slender, and cute.
Their eyes are sharp and they
    cannot wink.
Their complexion is fair and smooth.
They live forever and never grow old.
Only infants of less than a year can
    see them.
They steal an infant left outdoors
    after sunset.
They make the infant ill.
The infant fidgets and cries.
It is cured by being made to wear a
    black cap.

Why aren't babies allowed outdoors at night?
    _____ *They might catch a cold.*
    _____ *Babies are afraid of the dark.*
    _____ *Their parents fear the elves.*

The Tamawo

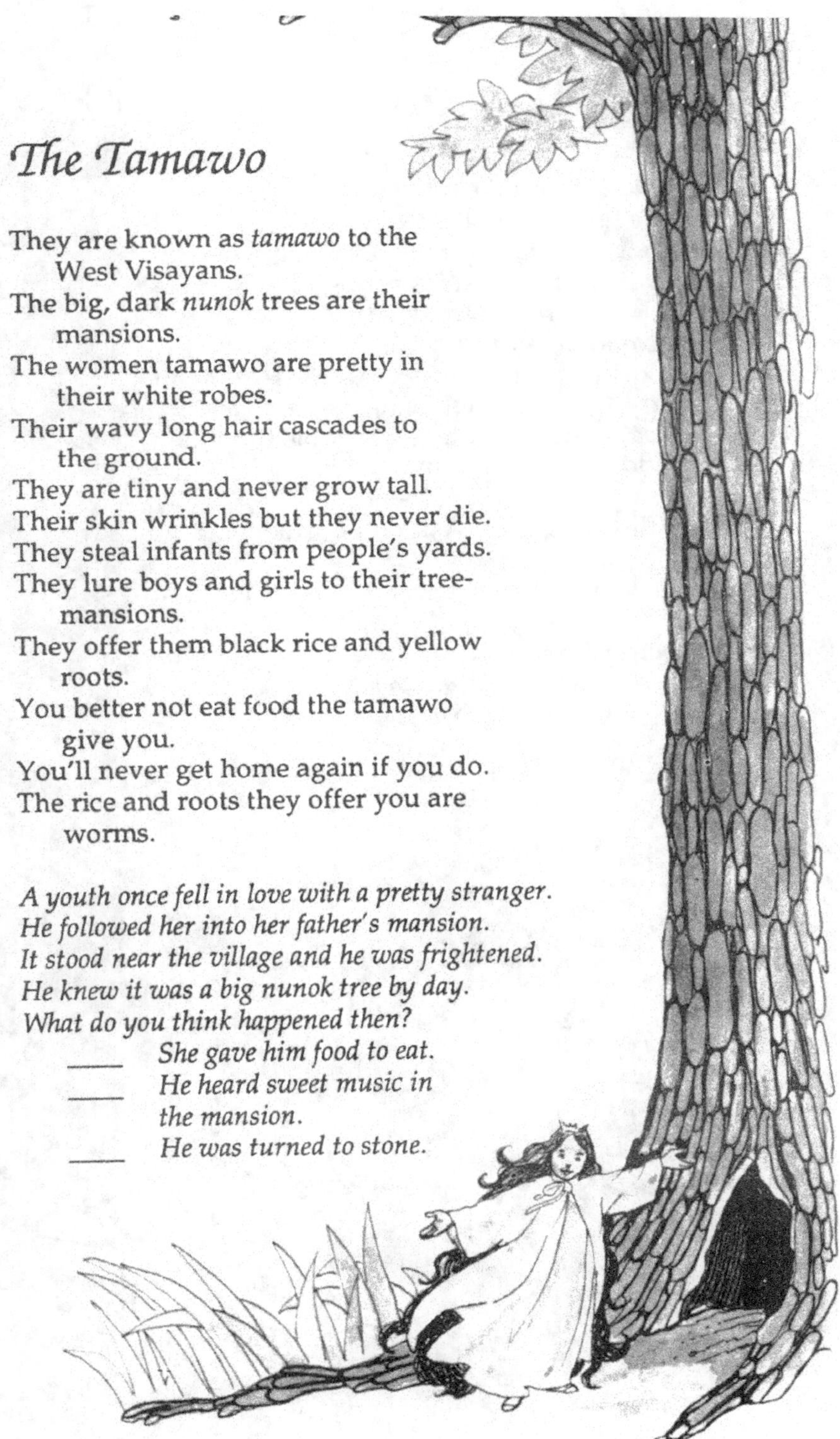

They are known as *tamawo* to the
    West Visayans.
The big, dark *nunok* trees are their
    mansions.
The women tamawo are pretty in
    their white robes.
Their wavy long hair cascades to
    the ground.
They are tiny and never grow tall.
Their skin wrinkles but they never die.
They steal infants from people's yards.
They lure boys and girls to their tree-
    mansions.
They offer them black rice and yellow
    roots.
You better not eat food the tamawo
    give you.
You'll never get home again if you do.
The rice and roots they offer you are
    worms.

A youth once fell in love with a pretty stranger.
He followed her into her father's mansion.
It stood near the village and he was frightened.
He knew it was a big nunok tree by day.
What do you think happened then?
    _____ *She gave him food to eat.*
    _____ *He heard sweet music in*
        the mansion.
    _____ *He was turned to stone.*

The Tirtiris

The Ilokanos gave them the name *tirtiris*.
They are little folk with teeth of gold.
They have long noses and a light skin.
They wear clothes of shimmering silk.
Their clothes are embroidered with gold threads.
They live in *bagbagotot* vines.
They skip and dance in people's yards at nightfall.
They like to be watched while they skip and dance.
They make friends with good people from the village.
They add rice to their bins.
People are afraid to hurt them.
When throwing things out of the window, people say,
    "Go away, go away."
People who hurt them get sore eyes and skin rashes.

Why must people say "Go away" when throwing things?
   _____   *They don't want to hit the tirtiris.*
   _____   *They want to be polite.*
   _____   *They are angry.*

The Ugaw

They are known as *ugaw* in Pangasinan.
They are as pretty as old-fashioned rag dolls.
They live behind rice granaries and rice bins.
They pound your rice in your *kul-ong*.
Their pounding sounds faraway, like an echo.
They move quickly and are hard to see.
They follow you when you enter your granary.
They steal some of the rice after you leave.
They steal rice from your bin, too.
They get exactly as much rice as you do.
Quickly cover the bin after getting some rice.
Be sure not to spill rice on the floor.
The ugaw will know where you keep your rice
    if you do.
Then they will steal from it.

What are the chief traits of the Philippine elves?
  _____ *They are all tiny creatures.*
  _____ *They are good-looking.*
  _____ *They live in trees and shrubs.*

The Ghouls

The ghouls of Philippine folklore steal human corpses and eat them. They have curved nails and sharp teeth for the purpose. They have a sickening smell because of what they eat.

Most of them look like men and women when they show themselves, but they are generally invisible. They live in villages by day. But at night they gather in large trees close to cemeteries. Then they go down and dig up the fresh graves.

They can hear the sounds made by dying folk from far away. They steal corpses from coffins and eat them. They grow more greedy when they smell a corpse. Then they snatch the living relatives, too.

The ghouls can be frightened off by fire, iron, and spices. They can be frightened off by loud talking and singing, too. Our ancestors kept a fire burning near the corpse to make the ghouls stay away. They hung sharp knives through the bamboo floor for the same purpose. They washed the corpse with strong-smelling balsam to keep the ghouls at a distance. Then they buried their dead right under the house so they could keep watch over it.

Some of the ghouls in Philippine legends are these:

    aswang as a corpse-thief
       (*various Philippine groups*)
    balbal (*Tagbanua*)
    busaw as a corpse-thief (*Bagobo*)
    kagkag (*Romblon*)
    paraduno (*Camarines*)
    segben as a corpse-thief (*Visayan*)
    ungo (*Zamboangan*)

The Corpse-eating Aswang

The corpse-eating aswang are ghouls.
The Bikols, Tagalogs, and Visayans tell about them.
They usually look like human beings by day.
Then they live in ordinary homes.
They listen for sounds of death in the evening.
They leave for the scene of death at midnight.
They steal the corpse and take it home.
They change the corpse to a pig on their way home.
They devour the corpse and feed it to their children.
They share it with their neighbors, too.
People who eat the corpse become ghouls.
Ghouls are afraid of spices and fire.
They are afraid of knives and vinegar, too.

Why does the ghoul change the corpse to a pig?
_____ So people can't tell it is a corpse.
_____ So it will taste better.
_____ So other ghouls will not eat it.

The Balbal

The Tagbanuas gave it the name *balbal*.
It has pointed teeth, hooked nails, and a long tongue.
It sails through the air like a flying squirrel.
It sits on the rooftop of the house where the dead lies.
It tears open the thatch a little with its fingernails.
Then it pulls out the corpse with its extended tongue.
It leaves a banana trunk in place of the corpse.
It makes the banana trunk look just like the corpse.
But the banana trunk can make no fingerprints.
Then the balbal carries the corpse home.
It gathers its family and they devour the corpse.
The dead one's relatives don't know their dead is gone.
They cry over the banana trunk the ghoul has left.
They make lots of noise to keep off the ghoul.

How can I tell if I am watching a corpse and not a banana
*   trunk?*
_____   See if it can make fingerprints.
_____   Ask the corpse in a whisper.
_____   Cry over it without stopping.

The Corpse-eating Busaw

The Bagobos call him *busaw* or *buso*.
Other people of Mindanao call him by these
    names, too.
Often he is a man-eating giant and is an ogre.
But sometimes he eats only the dead.
In that case, he is a ghoul.
He looks like a shadow by night.
He lives in large trees near cemeteries.
He digs up newly buried corpses.
Other busaw come to steal the corpses.
The busaw and their children eat and play
    in the cemetery.
They eat everything but the bones.

Why are many Filipinos probably afraid of cemeteries?
    _______ *They fear ghosts.*
    _______ *They fear ghouls.*
    _______ *They fear to lose their way.*

The Kagkag

The people of Romblon call them *kagkag*.
The kagkag live in the woods far from villages.
They hunt for corpses by night.
They put their heads in the mouths of mortars.
Then they listen to the other ghouls.
They listen at moonrise and moonset.
This is the time the ghouls all go to their feast.
They tell one another where they will have a feast.
They make themselves look like animals.
They smell like animals, too.
They are afraid of seaweeds and spices.

Someone was dying in Sidro's house.
The old folks told Sidro not to cry.
> ____ *They were afraid the kagkag would hear.*
> ____ *They hoped the patient would live.*
> ____ *They did not want to know the truth.*

The Paraduno

They are known as *paraduno* in Camarines.
They look like human beings.
But they smell like rotten flesh.
They roam at midnight looking for corpses.
They lie on their belly on the roof over the dead.
Their tongue sticks out as they listen.
They hasten the death of a sick.
People mustn't say a patient is about to die.
Otherwise the paraduno will make him die at once.

Why do ghouls smell bad?
_____ *They eat rotten flesh.*
_____ *They speak bad words.*
_____ *They are dead.*

The Corpse-stealing Segben

Visayans know it by the name of *segben*.
It is a ghoul if it steals corpses.
It disguises itself as a tiny locust.
It disguises itself as a long-legged frog, too.
It clings to the wall to see if the patient is dead.
It can't be caught because it jumps off quickly.
It has a sickening smell.
It disguises itself as a goat.
It has big ears that flap as it walks.
Its hips are higher than its shoulders when it walks.
It jumps quietly into people's backyards.
It pretends to eat grass there.
But it came to listen for sounds of death.
It hastens death by biting the patient's shadow.
It fears the smell of heavy smoke.
If fears spices and the clash of knives.

Why do some folk fear an insect or toad that they find in their
homes at night?
     ______ *They think it's a ghoul.*
     ______ *These creatures are dirty.*
     ______ *They want to protect the patient.*

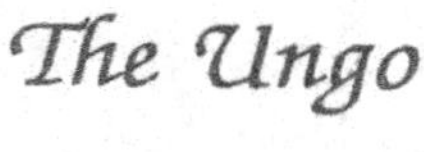

The Ungo

She is called *ungo* in Zamboanga.
She looks like a woman and sleeps all day.
She becomes a bird or a beast by night.
There is a secret hole in her roof.
She gets out of the hole about midnight.
She goes out to steal a human corpse.
She changes the corpse into a pig or fish.
She takes it home and cooks it.
Then she gives some of it to the neighbors.
Or she asks them to come and eat it with her.
They eat the human flesh and don't know it.
After that they become ungo, too.

What are the main traits of the Philippine ghouls?
_______   *They eat human corpses.*
_______   *They eat people alive.*
_______   *They smell like rotten flesh.*

The Giants

The giants of Philippine folklore are large creatures. Most of them look like men and women. But one of them looks like a bird and another looks like a monkey.

The villagers are scared to look at them. Yet giants do not eat people. Some giants even give fire to boys and girls who ask them for it. Some giants help the village fishermen. They lie down across a river till it gets dry. Then they call the fishermen to pick up the fish on the riverbed.

Giants live in crude houses not far from villages. They raise bananas, root crops, rice, and greens. They cook their own food.

But the giants are quite stupid. Children and even animals often fool them.

Many of the giants have names that people gave them.

These are some of the Philippine giants:

Angngalo (*Ilokano*)
Bannog (*Ilokano and Tinguian*)
Bekat (*Isneg*)
Bungisngis (*Tagalog*)
Buringkantada (*Bikol*)
Gisurab (*Apayao, Isneg*)
Ikugan (*Manobo*)
Kalapaw (*Isneg*)
Onglo (*Visayan*)
Sibbarayungan (*Apayao and Isneg*)

Angngalo

The Ilokanos gave him the name of Angngalo.
He lived in a great big cave in the Ilocos country.
His head touched the sky when he stood up.
At one stride he reached the land of the Tagalogs.
The earth shook under him when he walked.
The mountains are the earth he piled with his hands.
The seas are the holes he dug the earth from.
The lakes are his footprints filled with water.
But Angngalo was afraid of little red ants.
The people once crossed the sea to get salt.
Angngalo stretched his long legs across the sea.
They crossed the sea over his legs.
They came back with salt baskets on their heads.
Then red ants started biting Angngalo's legs.
Angngalo dipped his legs in the water.
The people fell into the sea with their salt baskets.
The salt melted and made the seawater salty.

How did the people probably feel toward Angngalo?
_____   *They liked him.*
_____   *They feared him.*
_____   *They hated him.*

The Bannog

The Ilokanos and Tinguians
    call it *bannog*.
It is a great big bird with strong
    wings and legs.
It can lift a carabao, a cow, a horse,
    or a man.
It carries them to its nest to
    feed its babies.
Its nest is on a big tree at
    the top of a cliff.
A man was hunting out in
    the woods one day.
A great big bannog swooped
    down and snatched him.
It carried him to its nest on
    a treetop.
The man hid under the baby bannog inside the nest.
He ate some of the meat the mother bannog brought.
The mother bannog brought these for its babies.
But the tree was very big and tall.

How did the man probably escape from the nest?
    _____ *He rode on the baby bannog when they*
           began to fly.
    _____ *He jumped out of the nest.*
    _____ *He climbed down the tree.*

Bekat

She is a giantess among the Isnegs in northern Luzon.
She lives in a dark cave not far from the village.
She cooks rice in a big clay pot in her cave.
She cooks meat in her big clay pot, too.
Two boys came to ask Bekat for fire one day.
They needed fire to cook a deer they had caught.
She gave them fire and secretly followed them.
She wanted to steal the meat from them.
She cut up the deer and gave them a little meat.
She put most of the meat in her big basket.
The boys stole the meat when she was not looking.
They put big stones in her basket and hid in a tree.
Bekat carried the basket of stones to her cave.
Her clay pot broke when she poured the stones into it.
She went to look for the naughty children.
She smelled this way and that and stopped under a tree.
The children sat high up in the tree by the water.
She thought the children were in the water.
She jumped into the water to catch them.
She drowned, for she did not know how to swim.

Why did Bekat jump into the water?
_____ *She was silly.*
_____ *She was thirsty.*
_____ *She was angry.*

Bungisngis

The Tagalogs call him Bungisngis.
He lives deep in a dark forest.
He looks like a big man with but one eye.
A long tusk sticks out of each side of his mouth.
His name means he is always smirking.
His upper lip covers his eye when he smirks.
His grin is widest when he sees a man he can fool.
He can lift a big carabao and throw it to the ground.
He is a bully but he cannot run.

You are riding your carabao in the woods one day.
Suddenly you see Bungisngis coming.
He is happy to see someone he can trick.
He laughs and shouts he will eat your carabao.
His upper lip covers his eye as he makes a big grin.
What should you do right away?
_____ Shake hands with him.
_____ Throw sand into his eye.
_____ Gallop away.

Buringkantada

The Bikolanos call him Buringkantada.
He lives in a big house with many rooms.
Vines with bright flowers cover his roof
    and walls.
Two little boys entered Buringkantada's
    house one day.
Buringkantada and his giant friends came in.
The little boys hid in the ceiling.
Buringkantada and his friends heard them.
"Who are you up there?" the giants asked.
"A giant bigger than you!" the boys shouted together.
"Show us a hair from your head!" shouted one giant.
The little boys dropped a piece of rope from the ceiling.
"Show us a tooth from your mouth!" shouted
    another giant.
The little boys dropped an old axe-head from the ceiling.
"Beat your chest!" shouted a third giant.
The boys beat a big bass drum with all their might.
The giants ran away and never came back.
The little boys took the giants' treasure.

Why did the giants run away?
   _____ *They were afraid to be eaten.*
   _____ *They thought the drum was thunder.*
   _____ *They thought the boys were a big giant.*

Gisurab

He is called Gisurab by the Isnegs.
His wives are Surab and Gungay.
He lives with Surab and Gungay in a cave.
Another wife of his is Sibbarayungan.
He lives with Sibbarayungan in his clearing.
His clearing is far out in the wilderness.
He raises rice and root crops in his clearing.
He has big granaries to store food in.
He stores up food for the rainy season.
He cooks his food in a big pot of clay.
Hunters come and ask him for fire.
He gives them fire, for he is a good friend.
He can smell them coming to his cave.

How do you know that Gisurab may be a good neighbor?
_____ *He gives fire to people.*
_____ *He can smell his neighbors.*
_____ *He cooks his food in a pot.*

The Ikugan

The Manobos of Eastern Mindanao call
     it *ikugan*.
Its name means that it has a long tail.
It lives in the branches of forest trees.
It is a great big monkey with a long tail.
Its skin is covered with soft hair.
It has large hands and feet.
Its hands and feet are strong.
It waits for its enemies high up in the trees.
It pulls them up with its tail.
Then it chokes them to death and drops them.
An ikugan was waiting up in a tree one day.
It was angry with some men.
They had tried to kill it with their spears.

Why was the ikugan mad?
        _____ *It was hungry.*
        _____ *It wanted revenge.*
        _____ *It was scared.*

Kalapaw

The Isnegs knew Kalapaw as a giant.
The people of Apayao called him Sappaw.
He was a very strong giant.
He could pull out a coconut tree by its trunk.
He could break the coconut tree on his knee.
He could walk past Apayao land at one stride.
He was too big to marry a human girl.
So he married his own sister.
His son wrecked the people's fences.
The people set bamboo traps to catch his son.
But he wrecked the traps with his little finger.

How would you describe Kalapaw?
_____ *He could appear and disappear.*
_____ *He was big and strong.*
_____ *He ate people.*

The Onglo

The *onglo* is a giant in the East Visayas.
He is big and has a frightful appearance.
His elbows and knees are as hard as stone.
He uses them to break shellfish for food.
The shellfish he likes best is the *tuway*.
There is plenty of tuway in swamps where the nipa grows.
So the onglo lives in dark nipa swamps.
It is cool out there, especially by night.
People can tell when the onglo is eating tuway.
They hear him breaking tuway with his elbow and knee.
They never go where the onglo lives.
They leave the nipa palms alone.

What really makes the sound the people hear?
_____ *People working in the swamp.*
_____ *Noise in their own ears.*
_____ *The onglo.*

Sibbarayungan

She is a giantess known to the
    Apayaos and Isnegs.
Some say she is the wife of the
    giant Gisurab.
Others say she is the wife of the
    giant Sappaw.
A man got lost while hunting in the
    woods one day.
He was very tired and came to
    Sibbarayungan's house.
She did not want her husband
    to find him there.
She was afraid her husband
    would kill him.
So she hid him in a wooden chest.
By and by her husband came home.
He sniffed this way and that way.
"There is a man in the house," he said.
    "I smell him."
"It's the meat you brought home,"
    she replied.
When her husband left, she let the
    man out of the chest.
She gave him food to eat and water
    to drink.
Then she showed him his way home.

How would you describe the Philippine giants?
    _____   *They are often stupid.*
    _____   *They are man-eaters.*
    _____   *They are big.*

The Merfolk

The word *merfolk* means 'people of the sea'. Merfolk are creatures of storyland. They are fish with shiny scales below the waist and good-looking humans from the waist up.

The mermaids have beautiful long hair and a light skin. The mermen have short, curly hair and a copper-colored skin. The mermaids are attractive females and the mermen are handsome males. There are few mermen but many mermaids in Philippine legends.

Philippine merfolk live in fresh water as well as in the sea. They live in lakes, rivers, and at the basins of waterfalls. They are fond of gold and precious stones. Merfolk living at waterfalls are said to be completely human in shape.

Merfolk do not usually get children to kill them. They imprison the little boys and little girls they catch and wait till they are big. Then they marry them.

Merfolk make their victims come near with their beautiful voices. They sing sweet songs or cry sadly. When people come near, they make the water suddenly rise. Then they get them and take them to their home.

Some mermaids come out of the water at night and call people to them. They join religious processions and whisper to a boy or girl, "Please walk me to the water's edge."

These are four of the Philippine merfolk:
kataw (*Visayan*)
mambubuno (*Zambal*)
sirena (*Bikol, Ilokano, Tagalog, Ibanag*)
ugkoy or siukoy (*Tagalog, Visayan*)

The Kataw

The Visayans call her *kataw*.
Her name means that she looks like a person.
She is a pretty woman from head to waist.
She is a fish with shiny scales below the waist.
Her skin is light, her hair wavy and long.
She lives in a beautiful house under the sea or beside a
      river, a lake, or a waterfall.
She sits on a rock drying her long hair.
She sings a sweet, sad song as she sits there.
She makes the fisherman row his boat to her.
Then she sinks his boat and gets him.
She takes him to her house under the sea or by a river,
      lake, or waterfall.
They marry and live together.

Why does the kataw sing a song?
_____ *She likes to hear her own voice.*
_____ *She wants to catch a man.*
_____ *She has lost her lover.*

The Mambubuno

The Zambals call her *mambubuno*.
She looks like a fish with a double tail.
She has large, black, slimy scales.
Sometimes her scales are of many bright colors.
She lives in a brook with a cave under its banks.
A fisherman can see her when the moon is bright.
He cannot help but follow her when he sees her.
He follows her into her cave and does not get wet.
Her cave shines with gold and precious stones.
She marries him and does not let him go.
He can leave only when she lets him.
He will drown if he tries to escape.
His folks will find him planted stiff in the water.
Or they will find him squatting stiff at the bottom.
But sometimes she lets him visit his village.
His folks do not believe the story he tells them.
They think he has become a fool.
Or he returns to find all his folks dead and gone.
A day with the *mambubuno* is a year among people.

Why doesn't the mambubuno let her man go?
_____ *She likes him.*
_____ *She hates him.*
_____ *She can't.*

The Sirena

She is called *sirena* in many parts of the country.
That name is a Spanish word.
People with a mole in their eye can easily see her.
She is a pretty woman from head to waist.
She has a fishtail instead of legs.
She lives in lakes, rivers, and bays.
She also lives in caves behind waterfalls.
Then she is a pretty woman without a fishtail.
She has long hair and a sweet voice.
She sits at the edge of the water by day.
She sings to make children come near.
By night she cries for help in the water.
Men go and help her, and then she gets them.
Or she walks on land and asks people to go with her.
Then she takes them to her house under the water.
People do not drown when she takes them.
But she drowns them if they disobey her.

You see a pretty woman bathing in the water.
How can you tell if she is a sirena?
_____ *She has a fishtail.*
_____ *She has an ugly face.*
_____ *She has a sweet voice.*
and a fishy smell.

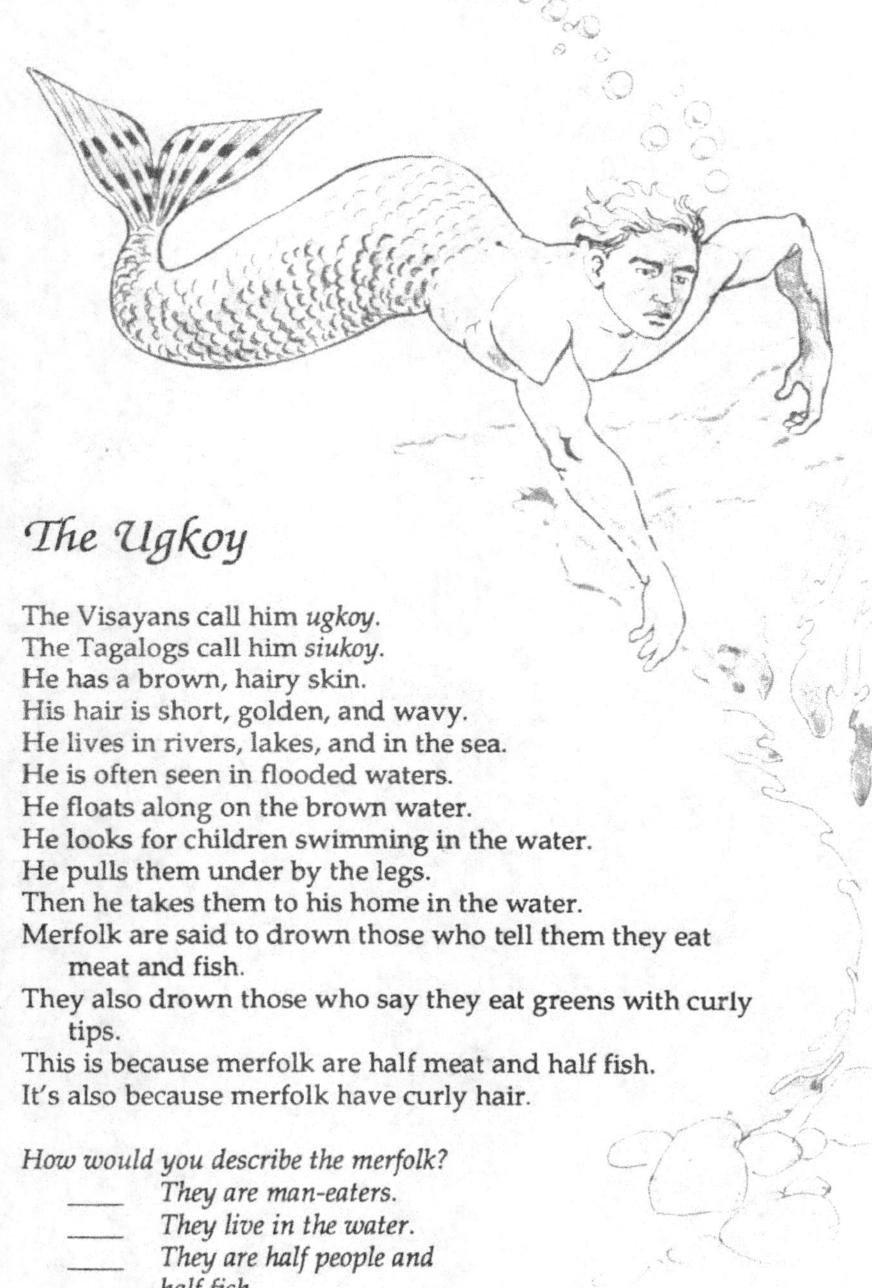

The Ugkoy

The Visayans call him *ugkoy*.
The Tagalogs call him *siukoy*.
He has a brown, hairy skin.
His hair is short, golden, and wavy.
He lives in rivers, lakes, and in the sea.
He is often seen in flooded waters.
He floats along on the brown water.
He looks for children swimming in the water.
He pulls them under by the legs.
Then he takes them to his home in the water.
Merfolk are said to drown those who tell them they eat
meat and fish.
They also drown those who say they eat greens with curly
tips.
This is because merfolk are half meat and half fish.
It's also because merfolk have curly hair.

How would you describe the merfolk?
_____ *They are man-eaters.*
_____ *They live in the water.*
_____ *They are half people and*
half fish.

The Ogres

The Philippine ogres are man-eating giants of mythology. They look like men, birds, and beasts. They are ugly and eat their human victims alive. They live far from human communities, in deep forests, and on faraway fertile plains. One kind of ogre has three big mansions standing on a wide plain under the sea.

Ogres are more frightening than giants. But like the giants, they often use fire and live in crude houses. There are some ogre communities. Ogres use crude tools and utensils. Some raise bananas, coconuts, papayas, rice, and sugarcane.

Many ogres can change themselves to birds or beasts. They take home their prey, both people and wild beasts. Like the giants, some ogres have kindly ogre wives who hide boys and girls from their husbands. Like the giants, too, some ogres have names.

Ogres are so stupid that children and even animals play tricks on them.

Some of the Philippine ogres are these:

alan as a man-eater (*Tinguian*)
Berberoka (*Apayao*)
Binobaan (*Ifugao*)
busaw as a man-eater
    (*Bagobo, Bukidnon, Mandaya*)
garuda (*Maranao*)
Inlablabbuut (*Ifugao*)
siring (*Bagobo*)
ta-awi (*Maranao*)

The Cannibal Alan

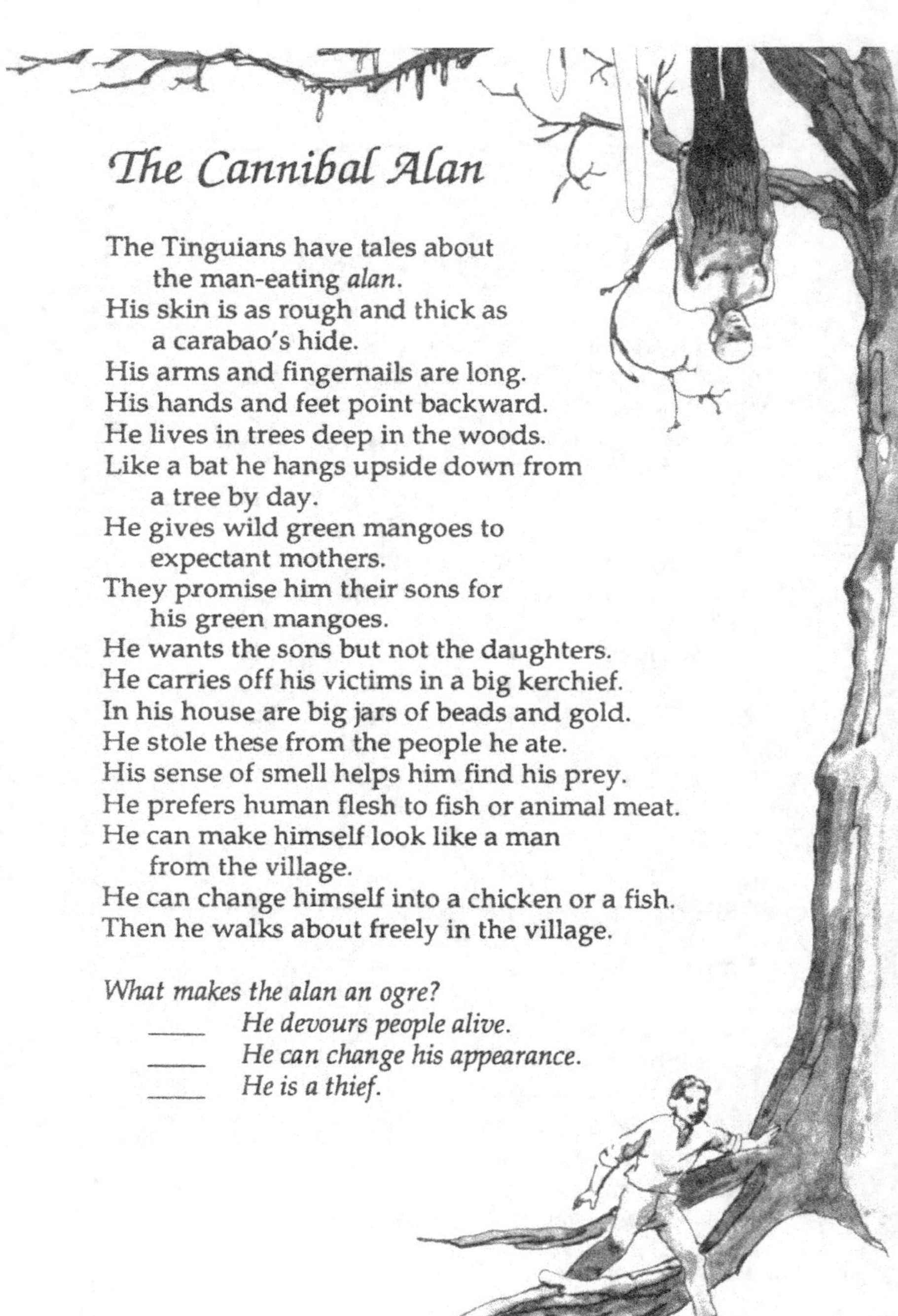

The Tinguians have tales about
    the man-eating *alan*.
His skin is as rough and thick as
    a carabao's hide.
His arms and fingernails are long.
His hands and feet point backward.
He lives in trees deep in the woods.
Like a bat he hangs upside down from
    a tree by day.
He gives wild green mangoes to
    expectant mothers.
They promise him their sons for
    his green mangoes.
He wants the sons but not the daughters.
He carries off his victims in a big kerchief.
In his house are big jars of beads and gold.
He stole these from the people he ate.
His sense of smell helps him find his prey.
He prefers human flesh to fish or animal meat.
He can make himself look like a man
    from the village.
He can change himself into a chicken or a fish.
Then he walks about freely in the village.

What makes the alan an ogre?
    _____ *He devours people alive.*
    _____ *He can change his appearance.*
    _____ *He is a thief.*

Berberoka

He is called Berberoka by the Apayaos.
He is fond of eating people alive.
He lies down across a river to make it dry up.
His body grows bigger to hold the rising backwater.
The villagers come out to pick up the fish.
They think his body is a dam across the river.
He suddenly gets up while they are picking up the fish.
The water rushes down and catches the people.
Then Berberoka picks them up and eats them.
But he is a coward and is afraid of crabs.
He runs home yelling when a crab pinches him.

Why does Berberoka lie down across a river?
  ____ *To fish.*
  ____ *To bathe.*
  ____ *To catch fishermen.*

Binobaan

The Ifugaos gave him the name of Binobaan.
He has a voice as loud as thunder.
He lives in a house in the farthest woods.
His house is roofed with forest leaves.
He stores up bundles of rice under the roof.
He cooks rice in a great big pot.
He invites lost hunters to enter his house.
He gives them rice wine to make them drunk.
Then they cannot run from him and he eats them.
His ogre wife is kind and hides people from him.
"I smell a man!" he shouts when he comes home.
"There is no man here," she replies.
He eats his dinner and goes out to hunt.
Then she lets the people out and feeds them.
She lets them go, showing them their way.

Why does Binobaan's wife hide lost hunters?
    _____   *To fatten them and eat them.*
    _____   *To save them from her husband.*
    _____   *To imprison them.*

The Cannibal Busaw

The *busaw* that devours human beings alive
      is an ogre.
The Bagobos, Bukidnons, and Mandayas
      fear him.
He looks like a frightful man or beast.
A busaw girl has but one eye just above
      her nose.
A busaw chief has an ivory horn sticking out
      of his forehead.
He has a big house standing on a wide plain.
His busaw followers live in huts around
      his big house.
They raise crops and domestic stock
      on the plain.
They raise bananas, papayas, and sugarcane.
They put on wings and then chase people.
The bones of the people they ate litter their yards.
But they are afraid of fire, brass, and iron.
Other busaw live in large trees in the forest.
Their hair is coarse and swarms with big lice
      and worms.
A busaw made itself look like a man one night.
He asked the cat at a woman's door to let him in.
The cat said, "Yes, if you can count my hair."
The busaw started counting, but the cat kept
      moving.
The busaw lost count and started again and again.
Then came the dawn and the busaw ran away.

Why did the cat move?
      _____ *To make the busaw lose count.*
      _____ *To keep warm.*
      _____ *To save her mistress.*

The Garuda

The *garuda* is a frightful
    ogre among the Maranaos.
He looks like an ugly man with
    a frightful face.
His teeth stick out of his mouth
    like knives.
He becomes a powerful eagle when
    chasing his prey.
His arms turn into wings and then he is an ogre bird.
Trees are uprooted when he flies over them.
He can carry six men in his powerful talons.
He has three big mansions on a plain under the sea.
A hole in the water leads to this land under the sea.
He keeps a pretty princess in each mansion.
The garuda took them from the kingdoms he plundered.
He also lives on the summit of a high mountain.
The mountain is surrounded by a heavy jungle.
He is crippled when his secret arrow is broken.
He dies when his secret bottle is shattered.
A young man once entered the garuda's realm
    under the sea.
He descended by a long rope his elder brothers lowered
He met the three princess in the garuda's mansions.

What did the young man probably do?
    ______ *He helped them escape.*
    ______ *He left them alone.*
    ______ *He married the prettiest and gave his*
        brothers the other two.

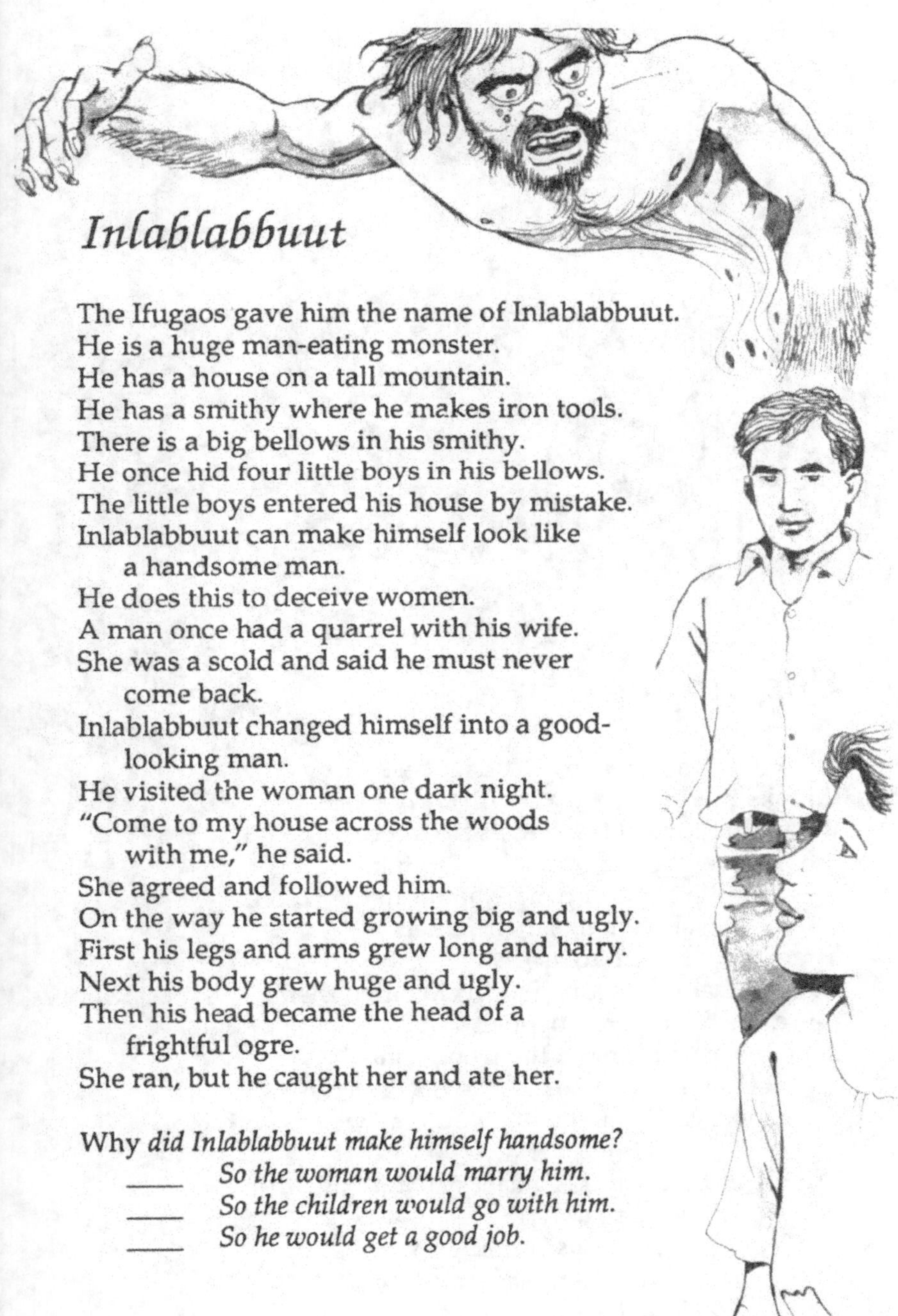

Inlablabbuut

The Ifugaos gave him the name of Inlablabbuut.
He is a huge man-eating monster.
He has a house on a tall mountain.
He has a smithy where he makes iron tools.
There is a big bellows in his smithy.
He once hid four little boys in his bellows.
The little boys entered his house by mistake.
Inlablabbuut can make himself look like
    a handsome man.
He does this to deceive women.
A man once had a quarrel with his wife.
She was a scold and said he must never
    come back.
Inlablabbuut changed himself into a good-
    looking man.
He visited the woman one dark night.
"Come to my house across the woods
    with me," he said.
She agreed and followed him.
On the way he started growing big and ugly.
First his legs and arms grew long and hairy.
Next his body grew huge and ugly.
Then his head became the head of a
    frightful ogre.
She ran, but he caught her and ate her.

Why *did Inlablabbuut make himself handsome?*
    _____ *So the woman would marry him.*
    _____ *So the children would go with him.*
    _____ *So he would get a good job.*

The Siring

It is known as *siring* by the Bagobos.
It looks like an ugly man with curly hair.
It has sharp, hard fingernails like a beast.
It lives in a big tree on a tall mountain.
It lures little children who wander in the woods.
It makes itself look like their father.
Then it leads them to its tree.
It feeds them with long worms to fatten them.
It is afraid of hot, red pepper.
A boy went hunting in the woods one day.
He met a man who looked like his father.
The man told him to go deep into the woods with him.

The boy wanted to make sure the man was his father.
What did he probably do?

    ____ *He crushed some red pepper.*
    ____ *He said, "Are you really my father?"*
    ____ *He said, "You are a siring."*

84

The Ta-awi

It is known as *ta-awi* among the Maranaos.
It is a monster with an ugly face.
It can fly faster than the wind.
When it approaches, it makes a noise like thunder.
It attacks villages and carries off people.
It eats them raw but cannot digest their eyeballs.
It imprisons pretty girls but does not eat them.
It imprisons them in its house on top of a mountain.
It is easily killed with a sword.
A hero once entered the ta-awi's den.
A charming princess met him at the door.
"Go away!" she told him. "The ta-awi will get you."
"I came to kill it and rescue you," he replied.
Soon the ta-awi came home and saw him.
The hero thrust his sword into the ta-awi and killed it.
Dying, the ta-awi begged him to open its stomach.
He did so and found a lot of eyeballs there.
He took them out and they filled a big jar.
He restored the lives of those the ta-awi had eaten.

What are *the chief traits of the Philippine ogres?*
_____ *They are easy to fool.*
_____ *They eat people raw.*
_____ *They make people ill.*

The Vampires

The vampires are blood-sucking creatures of mythology. The typical Philippine vampire looks like a pretty woman by day. But her tongue is long and narrow, like a drinking straw. It has a sharp point like the stinger of a mosquito. She marries a young man and sucks his blood little by little each night. She pricks his artery with the tip of her tongue and sucks out his blood. She does this night after night. Her husband dies for lack of blood. So she gets herself another husband.

Sometimes she flies out by night and sucks the blood of other villagers. In this way her husband lives long and she has a home in the village.

Some Philippine vampires die but come back to suck blood. They live in the woods far from human villages.

Here are the names of some Philippine vampires:

amalanhig (*West Visayan*)
aswang that sucks blood
    (*Bikolano, Visayan*)
danag (*Isneg*)
mandurugo (*Tagalog*)

The Amalanhig

The West Visayans call her *amalanhig*.
She is a dead woman who has come back to life.
Nobody would take her vampire power before she died.
She left her grave and now lives in the woods.
She comes to the village by night to suck human blood.
She sucks people's blood by sticking her sharp tongue into
    their necks.
Dying, she begs a relative to take her vampire power.
He who takes it becomes an amalanhig.
Then the amalanhig does not leave her grave.
When chased by an amalanhig, climb a crooked tree.
Her legs are stiff and she cannot follow you.
Or take a crooked path when she runs after you.
She cannot bend her legs to follow you.
Or jump into the water, for she fears water.

Why does the amalanhig have stiff legs?
   _____   *She's dead.*
   _____   *She's asleep.*
   _____   *She's made of wood.*

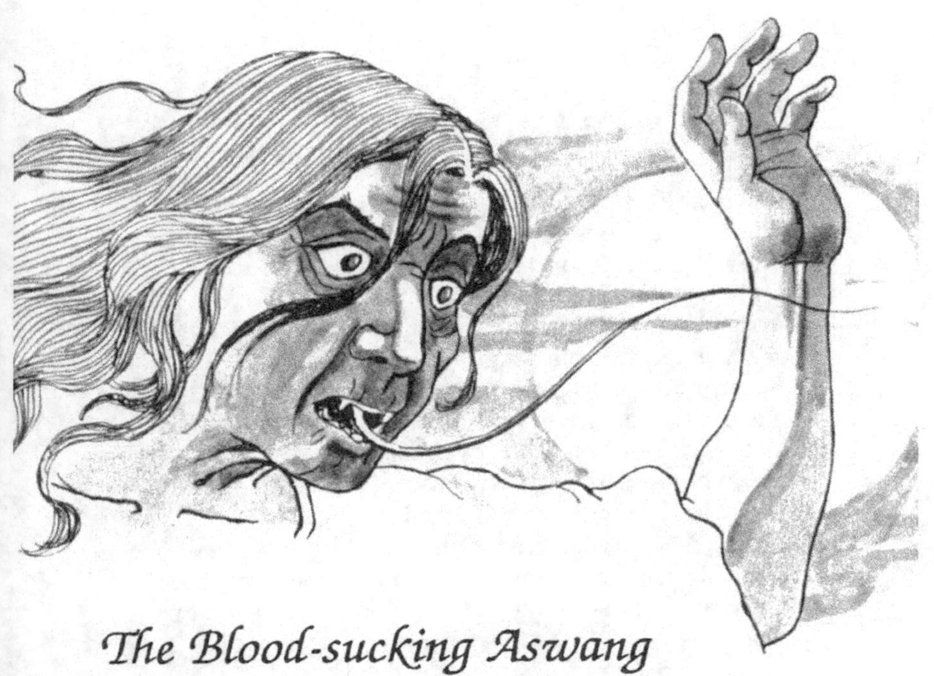

The Blood-sucking Aswang

Some Filipinos say there are blood-sucking aswang.
Some Bikolanos, Tagalogs, and Visayans say so.
A blood-sucking aswang looks like a pretty woman
    by day.
But she is an ugly creature by night.
Like other vampires she has a tubelike tongue.
Her tongue has a sharp point for pricking skins.
She lets fall her tongue through a hole in the roof.
She pricks a sleeper's skin with the tip of her tongue.
Then she sucks out some of the sleeper's blood.
She sucks out blood from different sleepers each night.
She looks like an expectant mother after she drinks blood.
She flies overhead crying, "Kakak!"
A night bird shows the way to her victims.

Why does the vampire have a long tongue?
_____   *So she doesn't have to get in.*
_____   *So she can tie her victims with it.*
_____   *So she can fly a kite.*

The Danag

The *danag* were gods of the Isnegs long ago.
They came down to earth and tilled pieces of land.
They planted taro in their clearings.
They became friends with people on earth.
A man was making a bamboo fence one day.
He was fencing his taro field.
A bamboo sliver ran under his fingernail.
He asked a danag to pull out the sliver.
The danag pulled it out by sucking it.
Some blood came out with the sliver as she did so.
She said that human blood tasted good.
She told her danag friends human blood was sweet.
They stopped planting taro and became vampires.
They lived by sucking human blood from then on.

What is this Isneg legend mainly about?
_____ *How the danag became blood-suckers.*
_____ *Why folks are afraid of the danag.*
_____ *When folks and the danag were friends.*

The Mandurugo

The Tagalogs know her as *mandurugo*.
She looks like an attractive young woman by day.
She is a winged monster by night.
She chooses a strong man and marries him.
She pricks his vein with her tubelike tongue.
She sucks some of his blood when he is fast asleep.
She sucks it between midnight and cockcrow.
She is very strong at that time of the night.
But she grows weak as the dawn breaks.
Then she can be speared to death with a sharp bamboo.
A laughing youth brought home a girl from the city.
He grew pale and weak and was dead in a year.
Another young man married the pretty girl.
He coughed and sickened and was buried in a year.
A third youth married the pretty young widow.
He hid a bamboo spear under their wedding bed.
He felt a tiny prick on his neck at midnight.
Then something heavy sat on his chest.
He made a quick thrust with the bamboo spear.
An ugly creature fluttered out of the window.
They found the woman's body in the yard in the morning.
A bamboo spear had been thrust into her chest.

What are the main traits of the Philippine vampires?
_____ *They eat people.*
_____ *They suck human blood.*
_____ *They can change their shape.*

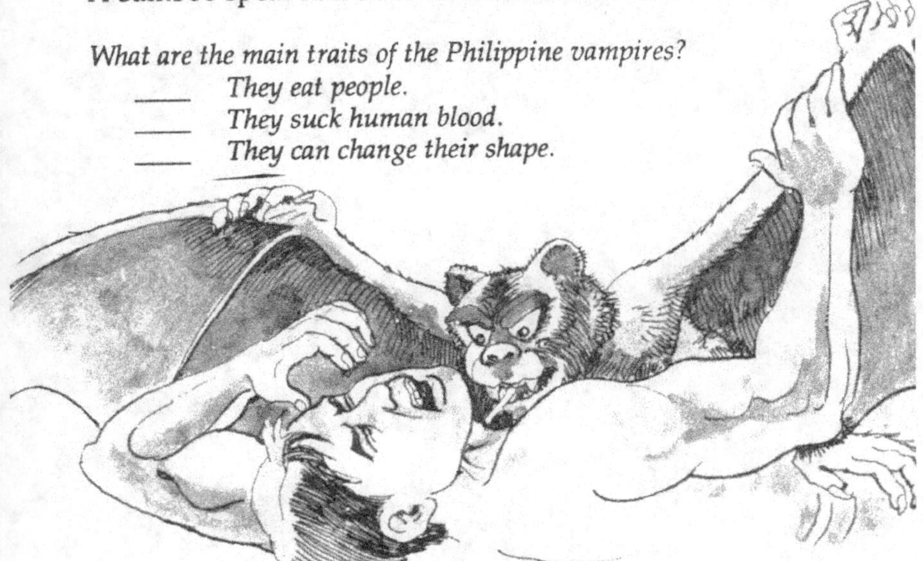

The Viscera Suckers

Viscera suckers are creatures said to suck out the internal organs and phlegm of people.

They look like attractive women by day, with fair skin, long hair, and pretty faces. But at night they become monsters. They grow wings in place of their arms and drop their lower body from the waist down. Then they fly out and sit on a roof. Their tongue extends itself and becomes a tube, like the tongue of a vampire. They look for a hole and let their tongue down through it. The tongue enters the body of a sleeper below. Then the monster sucks out the victim's heart, liver, lungs, spleen, and intestines. If there is an expectant mother in the house, it sucks out her baby, killing it.

The viscera sucker also hangs under the bed of a patient who spits a lot. Then she sucks his sputum. Viscera suckers are stooped because they stay under houses a great deal.

Some viscera suckers live in tall trees deep in the woods by day, while others live in lonely houses in dark woods. But most of them live in human villages with the men they have married.

They are afraid of knives, fire, salt, spices, big crabs, and the sting ray's tail.

These are some of the Philippine viscera suckers:

abat (*East Visayan*)
aswang that sucks internal organs
    (*Bikol, Tagalog, Visayan*)
boroka (*Ilokano*)
manananggal (*Tagalog*)
mangalok (*Cuyonon*)

The Abat

She is called *abat* in the East Visayas.
She is known as *awok* in other Visayan areas.
By day she appears to be a good-looking woman.
But by night she becomes extremely ugly.
Her eyes bulge and grow big and red.
Her fingers become long and bony.
Her lower body cuts off itself at the waist.
She covers it on the sleeping mat with a sheet.
Her arms turn into wings and she flies out.
She sits on the roof of a house she chooses.
She drops her tubelike tongue through a hole in the roof.
She sucks out the digestive organs of those asleep.
She sucks out babies from expectant mothers.
People close their windows to keep her out.
They hang the shells of crabs and globefish at the eaves.
They hang bolos from the walls and floor, too.
They don't go to sleep under the roof ridge.

Why do some folks refuse to sleep at the middle of the floor?
　_____　　*The abat's tongue is likely to come*
　　　　　　down there.
　_____　　*It's warm there.*
　_____　　*They want to sleep by the windows.*

The Viscera-sucking Aswang

Some aswang, it's said, suck people's viscera and sputum.
Many Bikolanos, Tagalogs, and Visayans say so.
These aswang are attractive women with long hair by day.
They live in homes with their human husbands.
They detach their lower body at midnight.
They hide it where it cannot be seen.
Their arms become wings and they fly
    into the night.
Their ears and streaming hair also help them fly.
They sit on the roof and suck the internal organs
    of those below.
Or they hang beneath the floor and suck
    the sputum of the sick.
They suck these through their tubelike
    tongue.
Sprinkle salt and ashes on the cut part
    of the viscera sucker's body.
Move her lower body a little to one side.
Or sprinkle vinegar or spices on it.
Then her upper body cannot join it
    when she returns.

Why does the viscera sucker
hide her lower body?
   _____   *So people won't sprinkle salt and spices on it.*
   _____   *So she won't forget where she put it.*
   _____   *So folks won't see it.*

The Boroka

She is called *boroka* by the Ilokanos.
This name is from *bruja*, Spanish word for "witch."
She is called *iki* by some Tagalogs.
She lives in villages or far out in the woods.
Her arms become wings about midnight.
Then she flies out to raid human homes.
She brings home the hearts and livers she steals.
She cuts these out of people's chests with her sharp nails.
She is scared off by the names of the things she fears.
People shout, "Salt and vinegar! Onion and ginger!"
People shout these when they hear her call.
She calls from above the roofs in the dark.
Her call is fearful to hear.

What probably makes the call which people hear?
_____ *A night bird flying overhead.*
_____ *The viscera sucker.*
_____ *Something wrong in their ears.*

96

The Manananggal

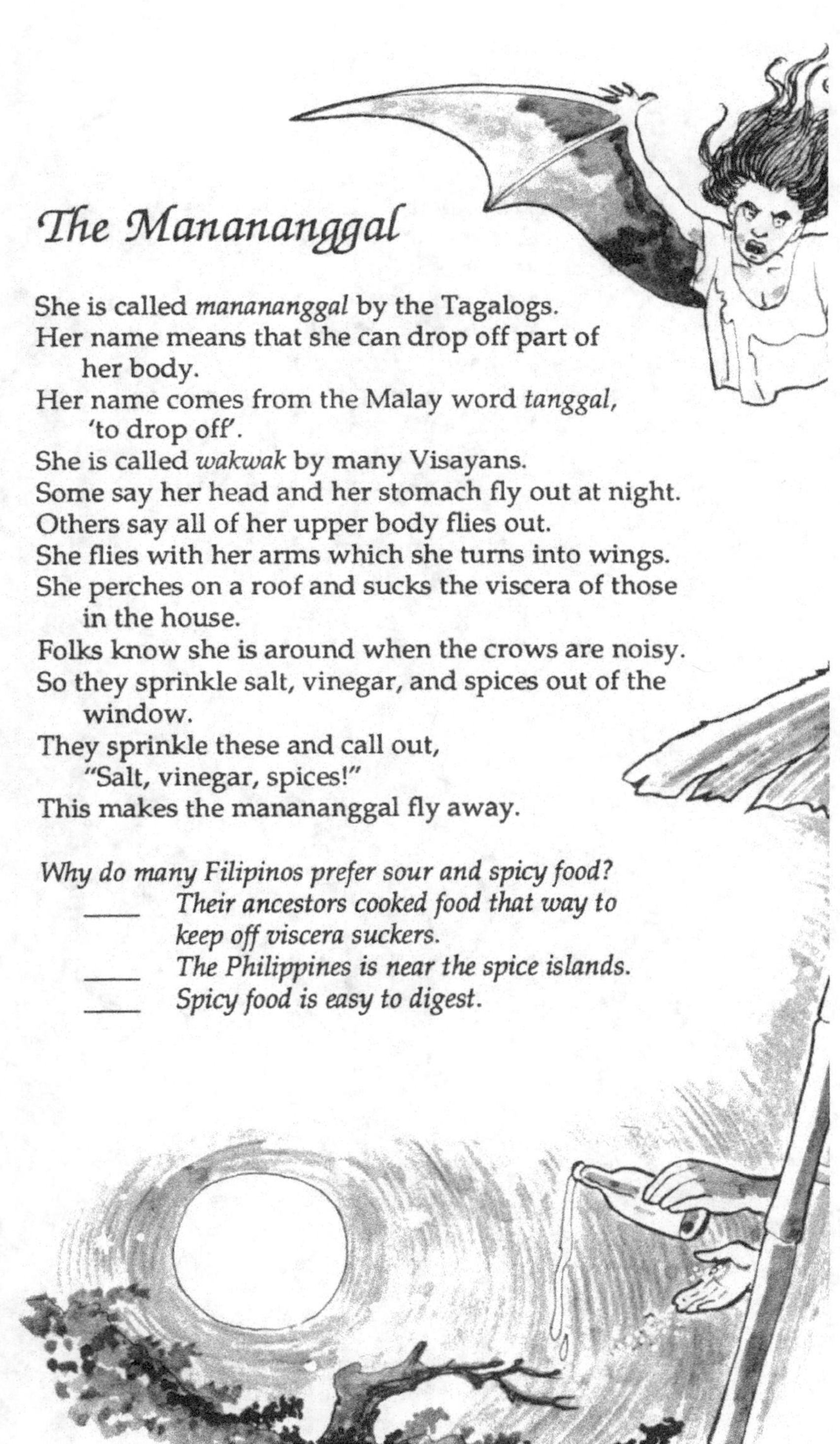

She is called *manananggal* by the Tagalogs.
Her name means that she can drop off part of
　　her body.
Her name comes from the Malay word *tanggal*,
　　'to drop off'.
She is called *wakwak* by many Visayans.
Some say her head and her stomach fly out at night.
Others say all of her upper body flies out.
She flies with her arms which she turns into wings.
She perches on a roof and sucks the viscera of those
　　in the house.
Folks know she is around when the crows are noisy.
So they sprinkle salt, vinegar, and spices out of the
　　window.
They sprinkle these and call out,
　　"Salt, vinegar, spices!"
This makes the manananggal fly away.

Why do many Filipinos prefer sour and spicy food?
　_____　*Their ancestors cooked food that way to*
　　　　keep off viscera suckers.
　_____　*The Philippines is near the spice islands.*
　_____　*Spicy food is easy to digest.*

The Mangalok

She is called *mangalok* in Palawan and the Visayas.
Some folks say she sleeps in forest trees by day.
She hooks herself to a top branch with her wings.
She drapes her long hair over her pretty face.
Then she sleeps soundly till nightfall.
She flies out to the villages in the dark.
Her favorite food is human liver and unborn babies.
Women with child fear her very much.
She sucks out the intestines of little children, too.
She steals the liver of a corpse on the way to the grave.

What are the chief traits of the viscera sucker?
_____ *Pretty by day and ugly by night.*
_____ *Eats people's internal organs.*
_____ *Segments herself.*

The Weredogs

Weredogs are mythical creatures who are men or women by day and turn into ferocious beasts at night. A werewolf is often the fiercest beast in a region. Europe has werewolves, China has werefoxes, and India has were-tigers. Since there are no wolves, foxes, or tigers in the Philippines and the creature is said to frequently look like a dog in this country, *weredog* is the most appropriate name for it.

Philippine weredogs are the true aswang. The name *aswang* is from *asuasuan*, the likeness of a dog.

Weredogs look exactly like people by day. They live in the villages, too. Toward midnight they turn into fierce dogs, hogs, and even big cats. They attack human beings without mercy. They sink their fangs into their necks. They devour human flesh raw.

They are afraid of the same things that vampires and viscera suckers fear.

The Philippine weredogs are these:

aswang as a ferocious beast
(*Bikolano*)
kiwig (*Aklanon*)
malakat (*Visayan*)
segben that eats people raw
(*East Visayan*)

The Beastlike Aswang

The doglike or hoglike aswang looks like a man by day.
He was a man before he became a weredog.
He became a weredog after a weredog breathed on him.
Or he ate a weredog's food by mistake and drank
      from its cup.
A chicklike creature entered his stomach and grew there.
The creature makes him crave for human flesh.
He attacks people walking alone at night.
His mouth dribbles when he attacks them.
He sinks his fangs deep into their neck.
He digs into their flesh with his sharp claws.
He is afraid of sour food and spices.
He is afraid of the thick smoke of burning things.
He is afraid of knives hanging between floor slats.

Why do beastlike aswang deserve our sympathy?
_______   They did not choose to be aswang.
_______   They beg us to pity them.
_______   Their appetite for human flesh is a disease.

The Kiwig

It is called *kiwig* in Aklan.
It looks like a stooped dog, cat, or pig.
Its tail arches down and then points straight back.
It has fiery eyes and tangled coarse hair.
It attacks human beings by biting their neck.
It kills people and eats them raw.
It fears people with loose long hair.
Women who travel at night must wear their hair loose.
They must carry garlic, onion, ginger, and lemons, too.
Then the kiwig will keep off from them.

Which traits best describe the Philippine weredogs?
_____ *They eat human flesh.*
_____ *They give presents to people.*
_____ *They look like fierce animals at night.*

The Malakat

He is called *malakat* by some Visayans.
His name means that he walks a lot.
He is a man who becomes a dog or boar at night.
His canine teeth grow into sharp fangs.
His eyes grow fiery and saliva drips from his mouth.
His nails become long, hard, and sharp
His elbows become thick and rough.
His hair crawls into his victim's eyes and ears.
It covers his nose and mouth and he cannot breathe.
The malakat bites his victim's neck and kills him.
Then he carries him home and eats him.

How does the malakat use his hair?
_______ *To choke his victim.*
_______ *To tie his enemy.*
_______ *To frighten people.*

The Man-eating Segben

The people of Samar say the *segben* eats people raw.
It eats their flesh after killing them.
It kills them by a mere touch of its tongue.
One cannot tell which end of the beast is head
    and which is tail.
It can run just as fast going forward as backward.
That's why some folks call it *umatraka*.
That word is from Spanish and means 'to move back'.
It prowls in village streets at night.
Its ears are round and large like taro leaves.
People flee when they hear its ears flapping.
They bolt their doors and windows tight.
They carry spices with them when they go out for a walk.
They carry sharp knives to keep the segben off.

In what way is the segben a weredog?
   _____   *It devours human flesh raw.*
   _____   *It can change its form.*
   _____   *It is afraid of spices.*

The Witches

The witches are the last group of Philippine lower legendary creatures we will talk about in this book. They may look like men and women, but they seem to be mostly women. They are extremely revengeful creatures. They make people ill or die. They do so by use of magic.

Philippine witches do not eat human flesh. They are quite shy and live in little huts at the outskirts of villages. They cannot look people straight in the eye, for their being witches can be seen in their eyes. The image in their eyeballs is said to be upside down. The irises of some witches are also thin and long, like those of cats and lizards in the sunlight.

There are many ways to fight witches. These make use of certain plants, the smoke of certain burning objects, certain objects in the home, certain practices, and certain sea fish.

Some of the most common Philippine witches are these:

aswang as a revengeful creature
(*Bikol and Visayan*)
mambabarang (*Bikol, East Visayan*)
mamumuyag (*West Visayan*)
manggagamod (*Ilokano*)
mangkukulam (*Ilokano, Pampango,
Tagalog*)

The Revengeful Aswang

The name *aswang* means five creatures in Philippine legends.
It means a ghoul if it devours human corpses.
It means a vampire if it sucks human blood.
It means a viscera sucker if it sucks internal organs and sputum.
It means a weredog if it becomes a beast and eats people raw.
It means a witch if it uses magic to make people ill or to kill them.
The witch aswang are either men or women.
They never change their form into birds or beasts.
They look sick and tired, and they have red eyes by day.
They are shy and live away from where other people live.
They cannot look people straight in the eye.
Their eyeballs are long and thin, like those of house lizards or cats.
They make people ill whom they hate or envy.
They put various objects in people's bodies to make them ill.
They make them ill by a word, look, or gesture.
They also enter peoples' bodies to make them ill.
The witch suffers if the patient is whipped.

When is an aswang a witch?
_____   *When she is revengeful.*
_____   *When she makes people ill.*
_____   *When she devours people.*

The Mambabarang

The Bikolanos call her *mambabarang*.
The East Visayans call her *barangan*.
She trains beetles, roaches, locusts, and moths.
She trains them to enter people's bodies.
They do so to make people ill or die.
She keeps these in a bamboo tube when they are at rest.
She sends them to attack her enemies at night.
They make her enemies' bodies swell and their skin burst.
A person who survives their attack becomes a
    mambabarang.

What are children likely to do if they believe in mambabarang?
   ____ *They enjoy studying insects.*
   ____ *They fear insects at night.*
   ____ *They like to play with insects.*

The Mamumuyag

The West Visayans call her *mamumuyag*.
She is cross and has a hostile glance.
She does not join groups washing clothes at the river.
She does not join groups chatting at the village store.
Folks do not pass by her house if they can help it.
They speak softly for fear of annoying her.
She gives various ailments to those she hates.
She gives them a twisted mouth.
She gives them painful tumors.

Why are beliefs about witches harmful to village life?
_____ *The people may suspect one another*
of being witches.
_____ *People who are not good-looking suffer.*
_____ *Strangers are not welcome in the village.*

The Manggagamod

The Ilokanos call her *manggagamod*.
The Pangasinenses call her *manananem*.
The Zambals call her *maniniblot*.
She goes out to harm her enemies when the moon is full.
She gives chills and fever to people she hates.
She keeps a tiny doll under her fireplace.
She pricks the doll with a pin where she wants her victims
    to suffer.
She picks up their footprints and roasts the earth.
She roasts the earth in a clay pot.
Then her victims will have a high fever.

Why do some witches have dolls?
    _____   *To play with.*
    _____   *To torture their victims.*
    _____   *To carry around.*

The Mangkukulam

The Pampangos and Tagalogs call them *mangkukulam*.
They look plain and are mostly women.
They live in tiny huts at the outskirts of villages.
People are afraid to speak to them.
People avoid them if they can.
They cause intense headaches, tumors, and pain.
They cause these by a wish or by pricking their doll.
They cannot go up a ladder with a pestle across it.
They fear the things viscera suckers and weredogs fear.
The mangkukulam avoid people, too.
They do not look people in the eye.
The image is said to be upside down in their eyes.
They pass on their witchcraft to their children.
Their children have no friends among the people.

Which traits describe the Philippine witches?
_____ *They can make people ill.*
_____ *They are plain and shy.*
_____ *They are man-eaters.*

Index

www.ingramcontent.com/pod-product-compliance
Lightning Source LLC
Chambersburg PA
CBHW050922260726
48660CB00001B/344